IS IT THEM OR IS IT ME?

A Guide to Practicing Self-Reflection and Accountability in Your Relationship

WRITTEN BY SAM SYLK

DEDICATION

This book is dedicated to those who have decided to examine themselves when it comes to failed relationships instead of blaming others. It is time to ask yourself the question, "Is It Them or Is It Me?"

CONTENTS

ACKNOWLEDGMENTS

I would like to show some love to my dynamic team for their help and support of this best seller *Is It Them Or Me?* My writing coach, Eryka Parker of Lyrical Innovations, LLC, my marketing coach, Donovan Boyd, Brian Artisan Photography, Elements of Style by Marchel'e, Burn Graphics, and my, barber Monte Garret.

I would like to thank my wife, Zenobia, who was supportive and understanding during this whole process.

I also want to thank my extended family: all the listeners of The Sam Sylk Show. I love and appreciate you all for all the love and support over the years.

FOREWORD

Who better knows about relationships than a man who has heard story after story of countless situations involving matters of the heart? And a man who speaks daily to hundreds of thousands of men and women who have experienced every aspect of a relationship? That man is Sam Sylk. As a radio personality for more than two decades, a father, husband, son, brother, and business owner, Sylk has heard it all, and I do mean everything! And that is precisely why he gives more than advice when it comes to relationships.

In *Is It Them or Is It Me?* Sylk digs into key underlying factors that determine what we need to realize about ourselves before, during, and after we become involved in a relationship in order to make it work. Using a sprinkle of humor mixed with a relatable and conversational tone, he makes it very plain to the reader the necessity of communication, trust, support, and recognizing red flags when figuring out the rights and wrongs in a relationship.

With every page turn throughout this book, your level of self-evaluation will increase, and you'll definitely start asking yourself, *"Is It Them Or Is It Me?"*

Bioncé Foxx, M.S. GSC

Radio and TV Personality

PREFACE

"Men do what women allow."

How do these words make you feel? Do they trigger something inside of you? If so, what? Take a moment to be honest with yourself, because if you aren't, how do you expect anyone else to?

"Hold on, a minute Sam. Slow your roll..."

I know, I know. I'm already treading on thin ice and we haven't even started this thing yet. But that's the object of this book. The definition of insanity is doing the same thing over and over and expecting different results. So, if we don't take the time to truly ask ourselves, "What am I doing now that contributes to the unfavorable results I'm getting", are we really using our God-given common sense?

Is It Them or Is It Me? is for grown and sexy adults who are ready to lower those blaming fingers and look further into the reasons why they find themselves in failing relationship time and time again. It's time to end this battle of the sexes and do what it takes to discover how the man in the mirror controls the destiny of our love lives and ultimately the pillars of the black community.

Now is the time to make a change in how our families are represented in society and how we are represented to the rest of the world. Seventy-two percent of black children are born out of wedlock. It's time to provide the self-healing and dedication necessary to break and rebuild the black familial cycle.

This book will either help you in your current relationship or end it. It all depends on your mindset going into it. Either way, you will move forward with your life and thank me later.

Are you ready, family?

Let's go!

INTRODUCTION

Many times, when involved in a relationship, we find ourselves playing the blame game. Whether we want to or not, we find it difficult to look at the role we've played when attempting to dismantle what has gone wrong in our relationships. We meticulously take the time and effort to examine how our partner has made us feel, but we don't take the time to set boundaries, ask the right questions upfront, or get past the fact that they "look good" and make us feel a certain way. Infatuation and getting caught up in a person's outer appearance prevents us from getting to know our mate. Some of us wait until they have moved in or we have parented children together to put effort into learning more about them. By then, it's too late.

Bouncing from one relationship to another before we have fully healed from the last one can prevent us from learning and healing, and often creates issues that we undoubtedly carry into the next relationship. We don't take a moment to realize that we might be the reason our past relationships failed. We may be too passive, stubborn, or caught up in pursuing the things we want for ourselves to see the warning signs that are right in front of us.

During my years as a radio show host of *The Sam Sylk Show*, I have included a staple segment called "Sam Sylk's Relationship Hour". Listeners from all over Northeast Ohio call in each day to comment on the daily hot topic provided by a listener who is experiencing hardship in their relationship and seeking advice. I also host couples' events that cover various relationship topics and feature open discussions on the issues that affect the average romantic relationship. I have heard every scenario, every outcome, and have observed various signals and warning signs of failed relationships. My callers share it all with me and my listeners, which triggers heartfelt responses and feedback from others who have experienced similar situations. One of the common denominators has always been that they are in too deep emotionally to see the situation with a clear frame of mind. They are unable to make common sense decisions because they have not taken the time to heal, reflect, and learn from their past relationships. But, it is the only way to break unhealthy relationship cycles.

Eleven years of marriage have shown me that taking the time to reevaluate your contributions to the relationship, remain open-minded, and have the willingness to change the things about yourself that are hindering the progress of your relationship are necessary to break harmful cycles. It also creates the healthy platform to pursue the type of relationship you desire and deserve.

If you're ready to learn more about how to attract a partner who is willing to love and support you unconditionally, is equally yoked, and is ready to commit to you, the remedy is often recognizing that it will require work and it's often an inside job.

It's time to ask yourself, *"Is it them or is it me?"*

SECTION I: COMMUNICATION

Getting to know your mate cannot happen without intentional and hearty communication. Verbal and non-verbal communication is happening all around us and at all times. We must make an active choice to interpret the verbal and non-verbal cues our mate provides us in order to fully understand their needs and expectations. Open communication is the key to growth, establishing and maintaining trust, and enjoying success in any and all of our relationships. This is why this is the largest section of this book.

I will begin with the fundamentals of communication, then expand into the complexity of communication habits in each gender. Lastly, I will explore how to create healthy habits to positively shape the impact that communication has on relationships. The first topic will touch on framing your mindset appropriately *before* you meet your mate. Without a firm knowledge of what you desire, need, and expect from your partner, you will never be able to adequately express it. Let's jump in!

TOPIC ONE

Setting Your Expectations

We're all familiar with the excitement that comes with meeting someone new and getting to know them in the beginning of a relationship. It's highly unlike any other and few of us are immune to the mystery and curiosity the early stages of dating can bring. The flirty texts, all-night conversations, coyness, and endless supply of attention and compliments can be magical...thrilling...and pretty damn dope.

We all move at different paces during the dating phase and that mostly depends on our previous dating experiences, beliefs, and upbringing. A combination of all those things can shape our views and potentially introduce baggage almost immediately after the "honeymoon period" ends. That's why it's important to make a list of the expectations you have of your partner and state them within the first three months of the relationship.

This is why I suggest enforcing a 90-day probationary period for new and existing relationships. The purpose of the probation period is to protect you from all the feels that happen in the beginning stages of getting to know someone. In the beginning, we often let our guard down or have our guard up too soon to realize the signs that are right in front of us. Actively set goals that align with your expectations of the relationship. For example, someone whose goal is to have an open-ended relationship is going to have a far different outtake on the relationship than someone whose goal is to get married in the next couple of years. By setting and expressing your expectations, along with setting monthly checkpoints, you'll be able to ensure that neither of you are wasting your time pursuing relationship goals that don't suit the needs of both parties involved.

In addition to setting monthly goals, focus on establishing a red flag list that consists of what you may consider to be deal breakers. By deal breakers, I mean qualities, characteristics, or circumstances that you're not willing to compromise on. Spend some time before you begin dating or in the early stages thinking about what you want out of that particular relationship. Determine at least three things that are deal breakers for you. It could be that your partner must have a relationship with God or they need to have their own household. Once you've set them, don't give up on your standards. You've drawn that line in the sand for a reason. Now, stand behind it with conviction. If you meet someone who does not meet your expectations, it's not in your best interest to begin compromising with yourself. If that's the case, why even set standards at all? There's a definition for that: settling. Standards keep you from settling for things that fulfill a temporary need but won't make you happy in the long run.

Additionally, be careful not to bark out orders or expectations in an abrasive way. The goal is to have meaningful conversations in which you bring up the things you value. You can do this by asking questions surrounding the issue to get your partner's viewpoint. If they stand on the opposite side of the issue, ask for more information. Remember to never dismiss your partner's viewpoint if they differ from yours. After hearing them out, calmly tell them where you stand on it. The key is not to set your expectations so high that they scare people off and you end up missing out on finding the love of your life as a result.

Below, you will find tips for setting the proper expectations in the first 90 days of a relationship that will give you clarity on whether it is moving in the right direction, as well as determining if your partner is on board with your relationship goals.

TIPS FOR SETTING AND APPROACHING PROPER EXPECTATIONS WITH YOUR PARTNER

Be mindful not to bring your baggage into the expectation-setting process. Leave the past in the past. For example, if the last person that did you wrong belonged to a certain sorority or fraternity, does that mean you should swear off the next member of that group who tries to get to know you? Is that being fair to yourself or the other person? Keeping an open mind while potentially entering relationships will get you a lot further than remaining in a place of resentment. Being close-minded will only inadvertently open you up to more relationships like the one you're trying to avoid. What you put out is what you will attract.

Try not to jump into another relationship right after a bad breakup. There's the saying, "The best way to get over one is to get under another." Not true, family. Calling up an ex, having a one-night stand, or doing something emotionally reckless is not going to lead you to the right person. Instead, you must try to take the time to reflect after a failed relationship in order to recognize the patterns you do not want to repeat. In doing this, you are educating yourself on what you want instead of focusing on someone else's needs. You're establishing your own ground rules and preparing yourself to receive the right person to have a drama free relationship.

Unconditional love is an expectation, but you can't experience that early on in a relationship. Instead, you can set a standard that your partner must accept you for who you are instead. The courting process should be taken slowly because you are learning about your new partner, which if done correctly and with care, takes time. If you're getting to know someone and they are judging you for your flaws the whole time, do you expect that to change once the relationship progresses? Recognize how they receive the subtle hints you may give them that aren't ideal and take a mental note for how they may handle the bigger issues later.

Know your boundaries when it comes to dating someone with baby mothers or fathers who bring drama to their life. They may not let you know this upfront, so be sure to ask if they are a parent and what their relationship is with their child's parent(s). If they gripe about the other person, take note that it may likely spill into your relationship. Then ask yourself if you are ready to deal with that? The same can be applied to you – if you have a baby father or mother with whom you aren't on the best of terms with, inform your new partner of the situation within the first 90 days to get their take on it. If there's drama, explain it in a reasonable way and allow them to make the decision of whether or not to stick it out with you. There's only so long you'll be able to hide it from them.

You should also think about whether you are okay with your partner still being friends with their child's parent. If they are extremely close and come over for the holidays to celebrate with your child and you know they have history, how will you handle that? The same applies to you if you are close to your child's parent(s). Let it be known early on so that conversation can be had, and any potential issues can be addressed and settled as soon as possible.

I've saved a rather controversial topic for last. It is important to consider the possibility that your partner may have friends of the opposite or same sex, depending on their sexuality. Many couples stand on opposite sides of the theory that long-term friends can maintain a platonic relationship without ever having or acting on sexual urges. There may also be cases where you or your partner remained friends with an ex. If you are uncomfortable with your partner speaking on the phone and hanging out with someone of the opposite/same sex, you should let it be known as soon as possible. This is a very common occurrence and the issues need to be brought out in the open early on to avoid drama later. If you wait until there are serious feelings involved and then try to hit your partner with an ultimatum, that's not only dramatic, it's also messy.

TOPIC TWO

Communication Obstacles

10 COMMON COMMUNICATION OBSTACLES IN RELATIONSHIPS

Healthy communication is the foundation of any relationship. The building blocks of that foundation consist of trust, understanding, and respect. How you communicate your needs to your partner is also very important. Without the understanding that comes from good communication, there can be no relationship. Point, blank, period! Let's take a closer look at some ways that communication channels are often obstructed in even the strongest relationships.

Lacking effective communication skills. Communication is a tricky thing that we can all stand to learn more about. In our mind, we may think we're a master communicator, but we're actually doing a sucky job. We may feel like we've communicated effectively, listened intently, and resolved an issue, but we have often failed to do so.

You may be asking, "How does that happen?" The answer is simple. You assumed you were a master communicator or that your partner is a mind reader. Most of the time, the wires are crossed without us evening knowing it. For example, you see your significant other in a new outfit. You like the way they're looking, so you decide to give them a compliment to stroke their ego. "Babe, your behind is looking thick in that dress!" She smiles politely, then heads back upstairs. When she comes back downstairs, she's in a different outfit altogether. Now you're defensive, thinking, *I went out of my way to compliment her and let her know she's looking good. Then she dismisses me by changing her outfit.*

But if you take a moment to think about the fact that she's heading somewhere to present to a group, you would realize that the compliment may not be appropriate for her to hear at that time.

Communication is an ongoing work in progress – especially in relationships. What you said to your partner while dating may not be what they need or want to hear while you're seriously dating or married. Knowing your partner and what their needs and wants are will help you build a foundation of healthy communication. Invest daily in perfecting communication with your partner in order to learn more about them and encourage them each day.

Being difficult to talk to. Your partner may not be able to tell you the truth because they feel you won't be able to handle what they have to say. For example, if they've cheated, they may think they can't tell you about it because you may still be holding onto baggage from infidelity you experienced in your past. Most of the time, this communication obstacle may or may not be due to something you have said or done. Sometimes repressed issues that your partner has not vocalized in the past can cause them to anticipate a negative reaction from you. The key to moving past this communication obstacle is to open up to your partner about your preferences when a difficult conversation needs to take place.

If your partner is tempted to cheat, do you prefer to know about it right away or only if the deed actually happens? Do you want all of the details, or only whether or not it has been resolved? As hard as it is to discuss things like this, it's important to be clear about what you want so your partner can openly express their challenges with you and vice versa.

Ignoring the fact that they're just having fun. Maybe you're just not the one your partner wants to settle down with. They could just be having a good time with you. We've all been there. You may come across countless Mr./Ms. Right Nows on your journey to find Mr./Ms. Right. They may view their relationship with you as temporary or perhaps, as just a phase. In most cases such as these, it's unlikely that their feelings will advance beyond that.

So how do you find out if that's the way your partner feels about you? Questions. It's all in the questions that you ask them. If they really feel this way about you, it is unlikely that they will hide it. So, figure out which questions about your current and future situation you need to ask in order to determine your role in your partner's life. The more direct your questions are, the better. Just be prepared to hear what they have to say.

- How do you think things are going in our relationship so far?
- What are your goals in this relationship?
- What is the next step for us and when do you want to take it?
- Where do you see us in a year?

If your partner avoids the questions altogether or is brutally honest with you about their unwillingness to commit, take it or leave it. If you're looking for something deeper and you know they are not, I strongly suggest you leave it. It's a waste of your time and it's very unlikely that you will be able to convert someone who is in this state of mind.

Lastly, make sure that you are honest about your intentions, even if it doesn't match your partner's. If they say they're just kicking it and having fun and you're hoping to develop the relationship into something more, you need to let them know that. Moving forward in the relationship with incompatible intentions isn't fair to either of you and sets your relationship up for potential failure.

Failing to hear your partner out. If your partner is the assumed head of your household, but isn't allowed to make tough decisions, that's a problem. Every household is different and I'm not telling you how to run yours. However, if you have agreed to allow your partner to lead and they disagree with your opinion regarding a household decision, they should be able to speak their mind regarding their concerns. The question is: are you willing to listen to what they have to say, even when their opinion goes against the grain? Or are you just rooted in your own opinions and beliefs?

Having an open mind and the willingness to collaborate and listen to your partner at all times is a very significant part of a healthy relationship. When the stubbornness kicks in, resentment, secrecy, and divisiveness aren't too far behind it.

Being "too independent". Before you start gasping and clutching your pearls...relax. It's okay to set the bar high for your relationship expectations. It's okay not to settle for anything less than what you feel you deserve. But you also need to understand that love is <u>unconditional</u>.

It's okay to say to your love interest, "This is my bar, you may not have to reach it financially, but these are my expectations when it comes to love and relationships. These are deal breakers for me."

In today's society, it may be years before some men can hit the same earning capacity as their woman, especially if they're blue collar workers. Today's workplace is different than it was even decades ago. According to the Journal of Blacks in Higher Education, "Black women currently earn about two thirds of all African-American bachelor's degree awards, 70 percent of all master's degrees, and more than 60 percent of all doctorates. Black women also hold a majority of all African-American enrollments in law, medical, and dental schools."

The fact is, sistas are viewed as double minorities when considered for positions, increasing their odds of being hired or promoted. So, if a recruiter targets a black college or association for a position within their company, they will almost always opt for the sista over the brotha if they are equally qualified. This is filling a double minority bucket, thus making the company look even better for it in the hiring process. Sistas, please don't look down on your hardworking man by comparing paychecks and career paths. If he is laboring in a factory or grinding as an entrepreneur every day, he is still contributing to the household in his own way while earning an honest pay. Remember: a bigger paycheck does not automatically make someone the head of the household. If ladies expect their man to be the leader, they must allow him to do so, regardless of how his paycheck stacks up to hers. Be mindful of making him feel like a man, like he matters, and acknowledge his contributions to the household.

As for men, don't allow your pride and ego to take the front seat if your lady earns more than you. You still have a role in the household as a protector and provider. Allow her to excel and reach her dreams without guilt or having to dim her shine. Be supportive and know your value in the relationship. Work together and be open in dialogue to keep the communication healthy and productive.

Struggling with agreeing to disagree. You are two different people with different life experiences, upbringings, and viewpoints. It is only natural that you will find yourself in disagreements from time to time. So, tell me this: does a difference of opinion lead to an insightful conversation or a knockout drag out argument?

It's important to feel like you're being heard when you communicate with your partner. If you don't, you will begin shutting down and keeping things to yourself because you have given up. But remember that it's equally important that your partner feels they are being heard. If not, the same will occur. When we stop communicating effectively, resentment, indifference, and even cheating can occur. At that point, you're faced with a whole other conversation. Do you reopen the lines of communication the right way or do you part ways? This is something that could have been avoided had you taken the time to listen to your partner's point of view.

Feeling it's more important to be right than to be compassionate. Have you ever let your partner talk you out of your initial instinct, even when you knew it was right, only to later find out they were wrong? If you're an open-minded individual, this can happen from time to time. There's nothing wrong with compromising or hearing your partner out. The problem lies in being disingenuous. Keeping the same scenario, what if you decide to call your partner out for convincing you to go down the wrong path by telling them, "See, I know I shouldn't have listened to you. You were wrong, again!"?

Listen. When your partner is down – especially after not following your advice or convincing you to do the wrong thing, you need to fight the urge to gloat and instead focus on lifting them up. Period. Think about it. Which is more valuable to you in that moment? Supporting them or taking a jab at them? Do you ever stop to think about how they may feel during a moment of failure, despair, or frustration? If so, do you immediately think of a way to support them or would you rather gloat about being right when they failed to see your point? Taking a close look at your priorities will give you the proper perspective on whether you're with the right person. The need to justify your thoughts is a natural reaction. So even if it's in your nature to gloat, the right person will inspire you to want to help them fix the problem together, rather than rub their failure in their face. This allows both of you to take responsibility, move on, and grow.

Faltering during adversity. The late great Dr. Reverend Martin Luther King, Jr. had a saying. "The ultimate measure of a man is not where he stands in moments of comfort and convenience, but where he stands at times of challenge and controversy." The same can be said about relationships. As a couple, do you stand strong in adversity or are you divided? When a problem arises within your relationship, do you communicate with one another or do you each form your own opinions or agendas and make independent moves? Do you check in with each other for feedback on how the other is feeling, even when you're mad?

These are habits you can form at any time, but it takes commitment to oversee every obstacle as cohesively as possible. It's you and that person against the world – not you and your mama, best friend, or neighbor. Your relationship isn't for social media, the gossip mill, or anyone outside of your union. Focus on keeping a united front, which will force you to speak to one another throughout the resolution process.

16

Holding grudges or throwing hurtful things back in your partner's face when you're upset. Family, this is a no-go – no matter the situation. It's necessary to think about the seriousness of this long and hard before your next disagreement. If you have been with your partner for a long time and have weathered a few storms, it's likely they have hurt you in a major way a few times. Whether it was by their words or their actions, they have probably cut you deep.

How did you handle that? Did you process your feelings about what they did or said to hurt you? Have you forgiven them and put it behind you? Just because you've chosen to stay together doesn't mean you've fully moved on from the situation. But...you still made the decision to stay. That's an active choice.

Do you still hold on to the hurt and resentment as collateral for the next big argument? Does your partner do this? If so, I'm about to tell you what you already know. That's not healing. You need to make the choice to be healed and delivered from your pain. Being delivered means that you are willing to forgive your partner. Some of you may be asking, "But what about forgetting?" My past experiences have taught me that, sometimes, you have to forget the pain as well. What purpose does holding onto it serve?

However, if it's physical or emotional abuse you are dealing with, then, you need to leave. Right away.

Focusing on your partner's shortcomings, failures, and areas of insecurity when you're upset or hurt. This is another tough one. In relationships, we often have to learn to accept the other person for who they are. Our love or support for that person gives us the motivation to overlook their flaws or habits that we don't necessarily like...until they piss you off. Then it's all fair game. Am I right or wrong?

Once your partner says or does something – whether intentional or unintentional – that rubs you the wrong way a few times, you might want to strike back at them. It's a natural reaction that you have to be mindful of to control. It's natural, but it's also inexcusable. It's always below the belt to name call, take jabs, insult, demean, emasculate, or ridicule someone else, especially your partner. It's the lowest thing you can do but it has the biggest impact. People rarely forget how you made them feel when the chips were down, regardless of how long ago it was or your intent. Telling someone the "cold, hard truth" as a favor to them falls into this category as well. If it's not done in a positive way, it's not cool.

So now you're familiar with the common communication obstacles. Hopefully, you've identified some patterns in your current communication habits that you can improve on. Remember, the goal is not to point fingers at anyone or place blame. The goal is to be accountable by recognizing ways you can improve the way you communicate. This is done to gain a better understanding of your partner's wants and to express your own wants effectively.

TOPIC THREE

The Art of Perfect Timing

The cliché "timing is everything" couldn't be any more appropriate when it comes to the topic of communication. Difficult topics should be expressed with an empathetic tone and delivered with sincerity. Putting a nice bow on a difficult subject can still prove harmful if the timing is off. Furthermore, it could critically damage a situation or relationship. With that said, our next topic will cover the importance of making sure that you are approaching a topic or initiating a discussion with your partner at the right time in your relationship. How do you know when it's the right time? That part can be a little tricky. There are multiple elements that go into timing that involve **intent, observation, patience, and knowing your partner's moods, habits, and rituals.**

Before approaching your partner, stop and think about your **intent** and whether you have underlying motives. What do you want to happen as a result of sharing this information with them? Is it to resolve an issue, to inform them, or to persuade or motivate them to take action? Will your news enrich their mood or bring their mood down? Even if you don't mean to bring down their mood, you can still do so by revealing the information at the wrong time. Waiting until they're happy to deliver bad news in order to soften the blow is self-serving. It doesn't make things any easier on anyone but the messenger. Overall, ensuring that you have proper intent creates trust, transparency, and stability in a relationship. So, tread lightly.

Next on the list is **observation.** Luckily, you have already learned about setting the proper expectations and having critical conversations early on in the relationship. If you follow this formula, there shouldn't be any information you're withholding that can potentially ruin the relationship. Remember, honesty is key in building trust in any relationship. Taking the time to learn as much as you can about how your partner receives and processes information will also help strengthen the trust in your relationship. What are their preferences concerning how critical information is delivered? How much time do they need to process it before taking the appropriate action? Do they like to consult others for input or work through issues alone? All of these factors play a critical role in how you choose to present information.

Patience when communicating difficult news is another important factor that cannot be overlooked. In order to master the art of patience, you must first practice empathy. As you know, empathy is the ability to view things from another person's perspective. By taking a walk in their shoes, you are choosing to open your mind to the way the world affects their thinking and thought processing. Patience has a big part in this because you may need a particular decision, response, or reaction from your partner right at that moment, but empathy causes you to wait for the right time to deliver the news. You may want to share the news in order to transfer energy, alleviate stress, or free up your conscience, but empathy and compassion will make you hold off for their sake.

When it comes to **knowing your partner's moods, habits, and rituals,** there is definitely a science to it. It may not happen while you are still getting to know each other, but that should not be necessary. As I mentioned, you should not have anything too critical to share in the beginning. This is why it's important to learn as much as you can about your partner's routine, how they prefer to handle the hiccups that occur in their life, and how those hiccups affect their mood. Knowing this will help you with determining the right way to deliver news that may impact them in a major way. For example, if you know your partner comes home from a demanding job feeling stressed and irritable, the moment they walk through the door may not be the ideal time to lay something heavy on them. On the other hand, if they are the type that likes to know what's going on immediately and doesn't like to be kept in the dark, then keeping news to yourself until "the right time" may not be the way to go.

Communication is never an easy task. We are all different and have diverse expectations, opinions, and needs. The best thing to do is ask your partner about their expectations when it comes to communicating and respecting their wishes. Add these elements to the batch and you'll have the right recipe for effective communication.

TOPIC FOUR

Interpreting Your Partner's Non-Verbal Language

Picture this. You've been stuck in meetings all day only to be met with a sea of brake lights during your commute home on the freeway. While fighting through the traffic jam, you get a text from your mate saying you're out of milk and a few other things. You stop at the store and end up stuck in line behind a person who wants to haggle with the cashier over the price of every single item. You finally arrive home and walk into your house, relieved and looking forward to an evening of relaxation – only to find that your significant other has invited friends over for dinner. Surprise! Have you ever been there?

I'm sure we all have. There's something to be said for a mate who truly understands you and can truly meet your needs within a relationship. Teaming up with someone who can not only empathize with you, but who also knows how to look out for you with minimal input from you is like finding a rare coin. Now, of course, no one enters a relationship as a mind reader. The writing isn't always on the wall and time and effort must be invested on both parts to get a true grasp on each other's wants, needs, and desires. That is why this topic is smack dab in the middle of the Communication section. You have to talk to your partner about what you want in order to get what you expect and need out of your relationship. It takes honesty, patience, and a mutual respect to learn how to complement each other and provide the support needed for fulfillment.

With that said, let's get into a few ways that you can ensure you are in tune with your lover's wants and needs at least most of the time.

HEARING WHAT ISN'T SAID: BECOMING FLUENT IN YOUR LOVER'S NON-VERBAL LANGUAGE

Non-verbal communication is very difficult to navigate, but will often give you a better understanding of what the other person is thinking and how they are feeling. By understanding the implications of body language, facial expressions, tone of voice, and repetition, you become more in tune with what your partner *isn't* saying. As I mentioned previously, your partner's choice to withhold information could be due to being uncomfortable, concerned, or poor timing. Below are some non-verbal cues that you should look out for from your partner while communicating. Identifying one or more of these may symbolize a need for further conversation or a little old-fashioned TLC for your partner.

Distrust or Disgust	Lack of eye contact, kneading their hands	Pacing or moving around	Defensive stance (crossed arms, lack of eye contact, stroking their face, etc.)	Leaning their body away from you
Nervousness or Anxiety	Breathing heavier than normal	Licking lips excessively	Using an elevated voice pitch	Being overly cautious or defensive
Stress	Isolating themselves from others	Using a short, clipped tone	Acting fired up, but in an panicky way	Acting erratic, more controlling than usual, or not delegating anything
Fear	Displaying widened eyes	Appearing stiff	Speaking in a tense tone	Licking their lips, holding breath
Shock	Displaying widened eyes	Opening their mouth	Raising their eyebrows	Leaning back

Guilt or Embarrassment	Displaying widened eyes, avoiding eye contact	Offering a plastic smile	Pursing their lips	Walking away during the conversation

Now, am I expecting you to be a psychologist or interrogation room expert? No. I know that in the heat of the moment, it can be challenging to detect and gauge your partner's physiological reactions. But, as time goes on, you will learn their patterns and eventually pick up on their needs. After you determine their mood and behavioral patterns, you'll have the opportunity to alter your reaction and administer a little care to help get them to a better place.

For example, let's say your partner is a tax accountant. It stands to reason that they may be unusually busy around February or March. While they may not come out and state how stressed and anxious they are, you can perceive this based on their display of some of the non-verbal signs above. You might want to hold off of having guests over or putting anything on their social calendar until tax season ends. If you notice the onset of stress on your partner, for the sake of the relationship, ignore some of the snippy comments, give them additional space, cook their favorite meal, or create a relaxing environment for them when they get home. If your partner has lost a dear loved one earlier in the year or around the holidays, you may want to give them a little extra attention once the fall hits, as it may be a tougher time for them. Gauge any mood changes that persist and ask open-ended questions to determine the cause. Remember, this is not the time to make it all about you.

For the sake of the relationship, it is best to try to ignore or downplay your partner's unfavorable moods during times of elevated stress. Be patient, exercise restraint and try to avoid questions that can potentially cause static during tense situations. "Did I do or say something wrong?" or statements that begin with "I feel like..." may cause your partner to become defensive or guilty for lashing out at you.

Remember not to jump to conclusions or project your assumptions onto them. If you feel as if their mood shift has become too much to bear or if you, yourself are having a bad day, take the time to pause before reacting or responding. Then try to establish as much space as possible between the two of you until at least one of you is ready to sit down and address the issue with a clear mind.

You may reach a point where you feel like you have run out of patience and that your partner's sour mood has gone on for long enough. That may be justified, because we have all been there. However, the most important thing is to find out what is going on with them. You can only do that by asking the right questions, holding a firm stance, then shutting yo' ass up and listening. This is key because what will follow is likely going to be an authentic expression from your partner that you need to hear. Now is the time to learn, not to be overly sensitive or make it about you.

TOPIC FIVE

It's All in the Vibes

Now that we've broached the topic of non-verbal communication, it's time to talk about a significant component of it that is rarely considered during our everyday interactions. When it comes to effective communication, positive energy and vibrations play critical roles in the process of connecting with your significant other. Google dictionary defines vibrations as "a person's emotional state, the atmosphere of a place, or the associations of an object, as communicated to and felt by others". Simply put, vibrations are the energy you put out at all times, whether you are aware of it or not.

Vibrations—we'll call them vibes for short—are all around us and compose all living and non-living things in our world. Higher vibrations are a direct result of positive emotional states such as happiness, excitement, love, and compassion for others. Lower vibrations are a direct result of negative emotions or states such as jealousy, resentment, hate, and sadness. The higher your personal vibration is, the more positive things you will attract into your space and your life. Positivity attracts positive components and negativity attracts negative components, with the exclusion of uncontrolled life events and circumstances. What you focus your attention on will ultimately manifest within your life.

Now that we've broken that down, let's talk about how positive vibes relate to your relationship. You can probably already guess which point I'm going to make, but let's dive into it anyway. When you are entering your lover's space – be mindful. At all times. Check your attitude, your mood, and your vibration level beforehand. If you have had a bad day and want to leave it all at the door, focus on what makes you happy—*before* you step foot in your lover's presence. Failing to do so will undoubtedly shift your lover's atmosphere and adversely impact the time you spend together. Now, I know what you're thinking: "Sam, what if I had a really bad day? Why can't I share that with my partner?" I'm not saying you can't do that. But, just be aware of how sharing that news with them can shift their mood as well. It all boils down to if you want to enhance their day or bring them down. Below, find some ways in which you can adjust your way of thinking in order to ensure your vibration is where you want it at all times.

IT'S AN INSIDE JOB: 10 TIPS FOR RAISING YOUR VIBRATION FREQUENCY

① **Be conscious of whom and what you expose yourself to.** Concentrate your attention only on the people and things that serve you and your immediate loved ones' best interests. Avoid the media, toxic people, and conflict to elevate your vibration frequency.

② **Infuse the habit of gratefulness into your everyday life.** Each day reflect on the things you have and want to have in your life. Take this opportunity to journal and concentrate on the things that are going well for you.

③ **Make time to meditate on a daily basis.** Clearing your head while focusing on your goals and the present moment play important roles in reducing stress and improving your mental health.

④ **Maintain a healthy diet.** Concentrating on high vibration foods like vegetables, fruits, and plenty of water aids in elevating your overall mood, health, and vibration level.

⑤ **Exercise regularly.** Keep a regular routine—whether it's taking a daily walk, going to the gym, or exercising in your home. It's important to stay as active as possible to maintain a high energy level.

⑥ **Actively seek out opportunities to help others.** Stay mindful of others' needs and how you can assist them. Volunteer and donate your time to local causes, demonstrate a random act of kindness, or call someone who is sick and shut in. It will make your day to make their day.

⑦ **Laughter and Smiling are the best medicine.** Smiling for only ten seconds can immediately heighten your mood. Just imagine what a good laugh while listening to the Sam Sylk show can do for you

⑧ **Forgive those who have hurt you.** I know it's easier said than done, but forgiving someone who has done you wrong or hurt your feelings is the best way to increase your vibration level. Letting go of any hurt, resentment, or ill-will will always do a number on your happiness level.

⑨ **Recite words of affirmation on a daily basis.** When you wake up, and throughout the day, focus on all the positive things about yourself and what you believe is going to manifest in your life. You can chant them, write them out on affirmation cards and post them around your home and at work or visit motivational websites. However you do it, keep it coming on a regular basis.

⑩ **Avoid the consumption of depressants.** Depressants such as alcohol and drugs are designed to lower your mood. It is important to stay away from consuming these elements in order to ensure you are operating at your highest frequency.

So, there you have it: a list of essentials for focusing on creating and safeguarding a healthy energy level. If you haven't already, actively practice maintaining a high level of vibration on a daily basis. It will not only change the way you view your relationship but it will also change how you view the world.

TOPIC SIX

The Do's and Don'ts of Pillow Talk

Ahhh, pillow talk – a very slippery slope. We all know that the post-climatic euphoric state can be a treacherous one. You've gotten your rocks off and you're snuggling with your partner, cuddling, and replaying all the details of the sensational lovemaking that has just occurred and, simply put, you're exposed. Completely and utterly exposed. Your mind isn't where it should be, you're not in any way capable of making any sound decisions and your guard is likely down. So, that's typically why this fragile state can be shattered by a few words.

"Tell me. What are you thinking?"

"Hey…I've been thinking."

"Can I ask you a question?"

Or worst yet: "We need to talk."

Yep, nothing can kill the mood faster than attempting to hold a pre-meditated discussion right after sex. Nothing. This is why you have to be mindful of the type of topics you choose to bring up post-coital. First, you should to check your intentions when broaching *any* subject after sex. Do you want to gain something through persuasion? Are you being opportunistic? Are you focused on a gain of some sort?

Intentionally waiting until after sex to ask for the things you want or to give your partner difficult news is another subject. This is a classic maneuver that's been around since the beginning of time. It's manipulative, sneaky, and not the way to maintain your partner's trust. He or she may not speak on it right away, but they will likely consider this to be an exploitation of their feelings and automatically assume that you have an ulterior motive. This may not only harvest suspicion from your partner, but it may also sow some seeds of doubt and resentment regarding your loyalty and overall intentions. Your self-serving intentions will likely be obvious, sour the mood, or even directly insult your partner's intelligence. At the end of the day, don't be that person who uses their body to get what they want.

Also, keep in mind that after great sex, your altered mind state may cause you to blurt out some things that you may regret. For example, you may have expressed to your partner that you weren't looking for anything too serious. However, after some good sex, you could find yourself saying "I love you" or that you want something more from the relationship than you actually desire. On the other hand, you may find yourself saying things that you do mean, but that are too premature. This will result in making your partner uncomfortable or turning them off completely. If you're unsure of the direction your relationship is heading in, keep the pillow talk to an absolute minimum. Trust me, you want to have this conversation with a very clear head.

Additionally, some people, for reasons beyond my comprehension, assume that that cool down period after love is a good time to disclose their infidelities to their partner. You will never get the reaction you are expecting by communicating with your partner in this way. If you are planning to confess any type of transgression or bad news to your partner (overspending, loss of a job, cheating, etc.), you should consider doing so with humility and respect. What could be more embarrassing and disrespectful than waiting until a shared moment of intimacy to do so? The bedroom is off limits for these types of conversations.

Remember that everyone we share our beds with may not be our soul mate. Listeners of the *Sam Sylk Show* have admitted to sharing personal information or details they shouldn't have after sex with their partner. If you are not careful, this could be used against you later or you could even be viewed as weak.

Lastly, when it comes to broaching the topic of marriage – you should wait for another time. Flat out. Pillow talk is not the way to bring up something as permanent as spending the rest of your lives together. This is something to be discussed with a clear mind and point of view from both parties. Putting it down on him or her will never be enough to get them to change their minds about making a lifelong commitment to you. If you have a pressing issue to discuss with your mate, please leave it out of the bedroom. Give the topic and your partner the proper respect when processing what you have to say.

A healthy habit is using this endearing opportunity to speak life into your partner. We tend to wait until a special occasion to tell our partner what they mean to us. The moments following intimacy are when your words will have the most impact. So speak from your heart and use this time as your chance to tell them what they want to hear not to pacify them or push your agenda.

TOPIC SEVEN

Are You Hearing Them or Listening to Them?

Have you ever heard the term, "You have two ears and one mouth for a reason" or of the 80/20 communication rule? Both of them have the same bottom line: you should be doing far more listening than talking. If you've ever wondered what the keys to a successful career, marriage, parenthood, and friendship are, it's listening. It's not about waiting until the other person's lips have stopped moving to speak your piece or nodding and smiling amicably to get them to stop speaking. Listening involves being openly receptive to the message being conveyed to us. More importantly, listening allows you to empathize and relate with others on a deeper level. Showing compassion and hearing someone out completely shows effort, trustworthiness, and concern.

"I HEAR YOU, SAM."

But do you really? Before you go skipping this section, thinking you're already a master of listening, let me clear a couple things up for you. There's a big difference between active listening and passive listening. Active listening is an art; it is something you have to practice on a regular basis to perfect. It requires energy, effort, and your full attention. So put that phone down. Turn that TV or radio off—unless, of course, it's during *The Sam Sylk Show*—and get ready to *listen to* your partner.

To listen without seeking full understanding is just plain hearing. If you receive your partner's words with limited interaction, their message will not resonate, and your communication will be blocked. There's no intention to empathize or relate with the speaker and you have failed at giving your partner the respect they deserve. Moreover, it's flat out dismissive and rude. Now that we've settled that, let's jump in.

There are five essential elements to the successful communication process: the sender, the sender's message, the medium, the receiver, and the receiver's feedback.

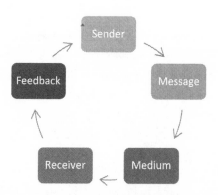

As you can see, there are a lot of ways that messages can become misconstrued during the communication process if we're not careful at each step. Active listening can help eliminate miscommunication as well as prevent you from repeating discussions in the future. And believe me, if the topic is important to your partner, you will find yourself revisiting it over and over. So, it's better to invest the time to address it in a healthy way now before it escalates to a far worse issue later.

Now let's take a step back. It all starts with the sender. They're feeling a certain type of way and decide they want to speak with you about it. So they create a message that conveys these feelings and send it through a medium. This is all good, assuming it was done correctly. They must first properly formulate those thoughts to describe how they're feeling, then utilize a medium that will allow you to receive the message loud and clear. In case you're wondering what types of media options you have available, you know I've got you covered – that's my territory.

You can break down media to either physical or mechanical. Physical media will more than likely be face to face conversation, video chat, or FaceTime, given the proximity of your partner. This is preferred because it allows you to pick up on the verbal and various types of non-verbal communication that are being used. Mechanical media is everything else: e-mails, letters, texts, direct messages, and those subliminal social media posts. Just kidding about the last one.

Now you can fully understand why the medium chosen by the sender plays such a vital part in the communication process. For the sake of time, we'll stick with physical media interpretation. When you are receiving your partner's message, you should focus on what is being said and how they're saying it. Observe the hand gestures, facial expressions, and tone of voice they use. These will help you actively receive their implied message. Take the time to process it. Don't formulate an argument. Don't take one thought and run off with it. Don't get defensive or make it about you. Just listen as objectively as you can. When you do this, you will be able to grasp what they're saying and understand exactly what they mean.

If something they say confuses you, ask a clarifying question *after* they pause. You can do this by summarizing or asking a specific question. That's your feedback, which is also a very important part of active listening. When you provide feedback, it gives the sender positive affirmation that you are listening and understanding what they are saying. It may also alert them that some of the signals might have gotten crossed and that there is a misunderstanding that needs to be addressed before the conversation advances. Either way, it's a step in the right direction regarding the health of the communication that is used in your relationship.

TOPIC EIGHT

Temperature Checks

Have you ever found yourself on autopilot when it comes to life? If you're like most people, you wake up in a hurry to get to work on time, bust your behind at a job all day, then rush home to cook dinner. You then put the kids to bed before squeezing a little bit of time in with your significant other. Then it starts all over again.

Well, I want to open your eyes to something you probably already know, but might have forgotten or simply overlook. In order to operate at a peak performance, our bodies need annual physicals and routine maintenance. Just like your car needs regular tune ups, your relationship needs frequent temperature checks to thrive and flourish. Often times, our perception is way off when it comes to the health of our relationships. That's only natural because you lack the ability to know what your partner is really thinking. They may say, "It's fine," but we all know that is not always the case.

A temperature check allows you to accurately gauge where you and your partner stand in your relationship. You may be under the impression that everything is going well in your relationship, only to be served with divorce papers the same week. It may sound dramatic, but it happens more often than you think.

In Topic Four, we discussed the importance of understanding your partner's non-verbal communication. Your partner's non-verbal communication often serves as an indication that a temperature check is needed on your part. There may be something happening beneath the surface of the relationship that needs some TLC. Some of the benefits of checking in with your partner on a regular basis are displayed in the following visual aid.

AMBITION

It is important to model a sense of ambition when considering the overall state of your relationship. Taking the initiative to assess your partner's level of satisfaction with the relationship requires the ability to think of someone other than yourself. When checking in regularly with your partner, you adopt a proactive attitude as opposed to waiting until something has gone wrong to react. You are taking an active role in preserving the health of the union by ensuring your partner is satisfied with *all* aspects of your relationship: sexual, emotional, spiritual, financial, etc. This allows you to tap into their mind instead of making assumptions on how the relationship is going. When it comes to being selfless in your relationship, taking a reactive stance is just too little, too late.

You may be wondering how to cultivate the ambition to check in regularly enough with your partner regarding the health of your relationship. The first step is to create a solid foundation that will only require maintenance. If your body has major issues, routine doctor's appointments won't be enough. The same concept applies to your relationship. If there are any underlying issues with your partner, take the time to focus on and correct them in order to sustain the long-term health of your relationship.

After you iron out your issues and return to a good place, don't just leave it there. Set calendar reminders to schedule time to sit down and discuss how things are going in your relationship. This is the time to bring up any and all things that may be bothering you. Take some time a couple of days before to think, journal, or pray about the state of your relationship. This will prepare you to lay it all on the table once the time comes to discuss your relationship with your partner.

TOPIC NINE

Relationships on Social Media & Screen Time

If you are involved in a relationship and are active on social media, you should speak to your partner and agree on the parameters and guidelines you will both adhere to regarding a few things. A few topics to address are the content you share online, your behaviors and habits, as well as your overall attitude toward social media as a whole. These are not topics to gloss over because social media has a large impact on our everyday lives and especially on relationships. Opposites usually attract, so more often than not, one of you is bound to be an introvert, tending to be more private and reserved. With that said, the discussion of how your relationship will be presented and represented on social media is key in fully understanding each other's boundaries and expectations.

First, you should focus on your primary reason for engaging with your audience. Then, spend some time thinking about why you choose to share content about your relationship on social media. Is it to inform? Entertain? Do you enjoy the likes and attention? Are you just doing it for the 'Gram?

We will explore how to give the topic of social media behavior the respect it deserves. Let's dive in.

UNDERSTANDING PRIVACY RIGHTS ON SOCIAL MEDIA

Posting. In the beginning of a relationship, privacy covers a wide range of components when it comes to social media. First, if one has a social media presence and the other doesn't, a conversation about whether both parties are fine with pictures being posted online is necessary. You or your partner's choice to refrain from social media use is intentional. So, before a picture from date night is posted, a discussion may be necessary. If both parties have accounts, permission should be sought out before tagging the other or sharing a picture in the beginning of the relationship.

If you choose to post a picture of you and your partner before you have agreed that you are monogamous, you may cause tension in the relationship as well as push them away. This will be a test of whether this is really your boo. Announcing significant life events such as a new addition to the family, or landing a new job or a promotion, for example, should also be discussed before posting. Don't let your partner find out what's going on in your life on social media along with everyone else. This is purely out of courtesy and respect.

A mother wrote in to the *Sam Sylk Show* and was very upset because her significant other posted a picture of their newborn child on social media while she was still in recovery from a complicated labor. She felt some type of way because the world had seen her baby before she did. Understandably so. Having these conversations beforehand can go a long way in preventing static within the relationship from developing. These practices help establish and foster mutual understanding and respect for one another's space and privacy.

When you are excited about being in a relationship, it often shows on social media. Boo'd up pictures, kissy faces, date nights, and special occasions are great to share with family and friends. However, posting only the highlight reel of your relationship can be problematic. Excessive posting can be overkill. For example, if you choose to post three or four pictures a week of you and your mate along with incessant "I love my man/woman" rants, there's a good chance your followers may begin to wonder if you're attempting to cover something up. Is it really as good as you say it is? Why do you feel the need to create a public billboard of your relationship? You'll notice that the likes will fall off and people will begin wondering what you have to hide. Remember, half the people that follow you are not genuinely happy for you and your relationship. Resentment and jealousy can harbor, and you may start getting unwanted attention. Less is always more in this case.

Also, if you are in a relationship, but you're "doing it for the 'Gram" by posting money shots, abs, booty, breasts, and thighs shots along with everything else, you should not be shocked when your partner takes issue with it. You need to ask yourself why you feel the need to post for attention. If you are lacking adequate attention from your partner, take the time to have a conversation about it instead of running to social media for the attention you lack. Posting pictures of that nature while in a committed relationship just makes you look thirsty and lonely. The relationship will seem weak to everyone from the outside looking in. If you are the partner of someone who was posting these types of pictures prior to entering a relationship with you, it would be in your best interest to take a step back and make a decision on whether you are willing to accept this type of behavior before getting serious.

Snooping. Now let's get into the next part of privacy that is a much more prevalent issue in relationships. Constantly sneaking to check your partner's direct messages, social media activity, internet history, location tracking results, text messages, email inbox, and any other personal activity is a definite red flag. If you find yourself doing this, you should eventually stop to ask yourself why you feel the need to do so. There has to be an underlying reason why you are compelled to check up on their every move when you are not around. Once you come to terms with this, you will be prepared to discuss the *real* reason for the distrust in your relationship. *Is it them or is it you?*

A brother asked for my advice one day because his woman read his messages, then went off on him for interacting with female friends on social media. I told him since the dialogue was harmless and consisted of things he would have said in front of his partner, it was time for him to have the boundary conversation with his partner. It's up to you to set expectations up front if you plan to create or maintain healthy long-term relationships. As long as you are respectful and don't have ill intentions, stand your ground. If it becomes too controversial, you will eventually need to make a decision.

Following Each Other With the Wrong Intentions. If you and your partner choose to follow one another or link up on social media, you should make sure it's for the right reasons. Tagging each other is cool and so is liking and commenting on each other's posts. However, if you're stalking your partner, tracking who they are engaging with, who they are following, or what pictures they are liking, then you need to reevaluate things. First, take a look at yourself and figure out why you feel the need to keep close tabs on your partner's history. Second, review the relationship history. Has there been a pattern of infidelity, body shaming, insensitive comments, history of exes, or other elements that have caused insecurity on your end? Is the mistrust the result the baggage you carry from previous relationships?

A female listener of my show shared an issue she had with her boyfriend who was following Instamodels. He had a fetish for curvy women and would sometimes comment on their pictures. At first, I didn't see much of an issue with it because the likelihood of him ever meeting the woman was slim to none. Besides, a like is just a like, right? Then she shared that he was still following his exes, who resembled some of those models. He had also made some body-shaming comments about her slender shape, small bust, and how she didn't quite fill out a dress like some of his exes. Herein lies the problem. I agreed that he should unfollow the exes as that was not beneficial to their relationship. I also advised her to have a conversation with her man about the effect of the belittling comments he made about her body. When there is history like this in the mix, it never ends well without healthy communication.

Hypersensitivity. Sometimes it boils down to being far too sensitive about things. Being sensitive and insecure does not always have to do with baggage or issues within the relationship. In today's society, fake lashes, hair, busts, and butts, filters, Photoshop, and contour, are everywhere we look. How are women supposed to honestly compete with that? While this is understandable, you must also admit that you have to come to terms with the fact that your partner is with you for what only you can bring to the table.

If you are feeling insecure about your partner's social media activity, you are going to have a long road ahead of you. Communication, mutual respect, and understanding is far more valuable in a relationship than jealousy, envy, and insecurity. If something is bothering you, talk about it. It's only then that you will be able to determine whether you have a real cause for concern regarding your partner's intentions and social media conduct.

SCREEN TIME VERSUS QUALITY TIME

Nothing ruins a one-on-one vibe like the sound of a ping. Many of the communication issues that exist in relationships today are due to the immense increase in screen activity on our electronic devices over the years. According to Flurry Analytics' research study, we are spending at least five hours on our phones **each day**. Whether we are checking emails on our tablet, reading articles on our laptop, or scrolling on social media feeds or texting on our phones, we are often fully engaged with an inanimate object far more frequently than with our loved ones. This includes our children, partners, friends, and other loved ones. Sad.

Now that we have a number to work with, let's add on eight hours of work and one to two hours of commuting back and forth. That only leaves nine to ten hours left for sleep and interaction with loved ones. In the greater scope, five hours of staring at a phone for personal entertainment sounds absurd. Nevertheless, we still continue to keep our handheld devices in tow as we eat dinner, watch television, go on date nights, take the kids to the playground, or any other social activities we engage in. Many of us don't even let operating two thousand pounds of steel while driving every day interfere with our texting and scrolling, which is dangerous, reckless, and sad.

Let's take a look at some of the ways we are becoming more and more disconnected from the people we care about due to uncontrollable FOMO (fear of missing out). Below, I have listed some of the barriers we have created due to excessive phone use.

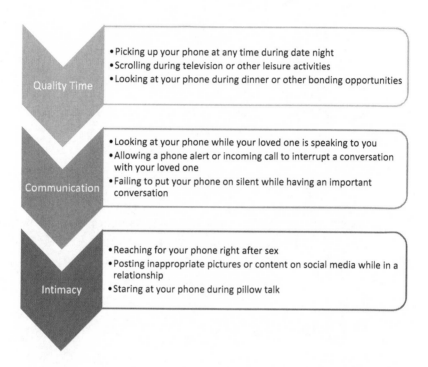

Quality Time
- Picking up your phone at any time during date night
- Scrolling during television or other leisure activities
- Looking at your phone during dinner or other bonding opportunities

Communication
- Looking at your phone while your loved one is speaking to you
- Allowing a phone alert or incoming call to interrupt a conversation with your loved one
- Failing to put your phone on silent while having an important conversation

Intimacy
- Reaching for your phone right after sex
- Posting inappropriate pictures or content on social media while in a relationship
- Staring at your phone during pillow talk

The bottom line is this, overuse of phones and other personal electronics create a wedge between ourselves and others. Be cognizant of when you use social media and your phone and what the opportunity cost will be. What are you giving up in order to scroll, text, or read? What's right in front of you or next to you? What's more important to your livelihood and theirs?

Be accessible to your partner. Engage with your partner. Be mindful of your interactions and the impact of your actions on your loved ones. Be intentional with your purpose and your impact. Don't allow fleeting, insignificant moments and obligational urges drive a wall between you and the ones you love. Just put the phone down.

TOPIC TEN

Gender Language Barriers

Gender language barriers can greatly affect the dynamics of your relationship. You've probably heard the saying that men are from Mars and women are from Venus. Sometimes, during conversations with your significant other, it can feel like the saying has some truth to it. Men and women have distinct ways of thinking and communicating with others. In general, both sexes tend to have a different approach to many of life's circumstances. One of the more glaring differences is the way we communicate with members of the opposite sex, which can often lead to gross misconceptions, frustrations, and discord within the relationship.

Taking a closer look at how males and females think and express themselves can help shed some light on the underlying causes of rifts that may appear in the relationship over time. Over the span of my life, I have encountered various barriers when communicating with the opposite sex. In my communication with females, I have often needed to step back to evaluate my way of communicating to ensure my message was clear and appropriately received. Intention means nothing, perception is everything.

WOMEN

When exploring the intent of communication from a female's perspective, it's important to note that their natural disposition is to preserve healthy and positive relationships in their lives. This is where women thrive – feeling as if the ones they love are in harmony and on one accord with them. Women seek to be heard and listen to others to ensure a sense of mutual understanding. Balance is important to a woman in order to function properly, as it is often difficult for them to move forward if they feel there are any loose ends present. A woman operates from a collaborative and empathetic frame of mind, actively seeking out the advisement of her peers regarding decision making. She craves stability and plans ahead to make sure her needs and the needs of her loved ones are accounted for.

When it comes to conflict, females seek to discuss the issue in depth. They want to explore and resolve the conflict to make sure it is fully addressed and that it will not arise again. This ties in with the female's preventive nature. If a woman presents an issue to her partner, she will likely want to discuss it at length to gain clarity before attempting to resolve it.

When it comes to relationships, some females have the tendency to evaluate each candidate for relationship potential. Note, this may not be the case for those who are happily single or who are not actively looking for a relationship. However, if a sista meets a viable male, she will immediately begin sizing him up against her standards to see if he is a good match.

MEN

Males, on the other hand, have a natural disposition to focus on our responsibilities. Our nature urges us to protect and provide for our family, which lessens our focus on preservation. Our analytical and solution-oriented nature makes it challenging to consult others during decision making. We see this as unnecessary and a waste of time. We don't ask questions or look to dive deeper into issues collaboratively, but find ways to address issues independently. Our goal is to tie up any loose ends as quickly and efficiently as possible. We operate from a fact-seeking frame of mind and actively seek solutions in order to advise others regarding the decision-making process.

When it comes to conflict, we tend to internalize our thoughts and feelings about the issue. We prefer to resolve conflict quickly and move forward by thinking things through. We prefer not to hash out the details verbally. If a woman presents an issue to her male partner, he will likely want to squash it by immediately attempting to resolve it.

As males, elaborating on our feelings, innermost thoughts, and fears is not natural or socially appropriate. We tend to internalize what we experience on a daily basis, concealing the sense of pressure, worry, and doubt that we have about everyday things. When our counterpart is hurting and is verbally expressive about it, we tend to resist sharing our own feelings about the situation. We may lash out instead, due to bottling up all of the stress that we are experiencing. Some of us were taught not to cry or show any sign of weakness, hence the communication barrier is established.

When it comes to relationships, men tend to have a different set of standards. Males have needs that often fall within one or more of four categories: pursue, protect, provide, and penetrate. Think about it this way: a man may see a woman who is attractive and is sending out the right vibes. His main goal is to pursue her – to get to know her better and find out as much as he can about her. He may also have a home girl that he's known since elementary school who has become just like a sister to him over the years. His basic instinct is to protect her at all costs instead of pursuing her romantically. While out kicking it with friends, he may come across a female who is giving him all types of sexual vibes. She's openly flirting with him and sending him signals all night. His agenda will be to sleep with her, as quickly as possible. This could easily be the same woman in all three scenarios. But it all depends on how she conducts herself.

Some guys enjoy the pursuit of a woman just for the sport of it. The first P is **pursuit**. Pursuit is an innate need for males. In that need, we may not have the "why" figured out at first. Simply put, there is a challenge involved in the pursuit and it all depends on how a female presents herself. This is why females have to be mindful of how they dress, talk, and act around the opposite sex. If the energy that women emit attracts unsavory people, it's normally due to their own underlying energy or intentions.

So you may be wondering, *what does pursuit entail from a male's perspective?* I'm so glad you asked. In a nutshell, pursuit involves intrigue, interest, curiosity, and the fascination of getting to know another individual. Pursuit could begin with a physical attraction or lust, but it doesn't always end there. It may go a bit deeper. A genuine interest in getting to know someone on an intimate or romantic level is a part of pursuit as well. In the past, have you ever seen someone at work, at church, or around the neighborhood who piqued your interest? If so, the next step you take toward getting to know them can be defined as pursuit. A male may introduce himself, ask for her number, slide in her DMs, ask a mutual friend about her, etc. As I mentioned before, the "why" is not always at the forefront. He may want to just penetrate or he may want to make her wifey. It all depends on where he is in his life and the type of vibes she sends out. Ladies, just concentrate on being yourself in order to attract the type of attention you want in your life. When the interest is there, the communication commences.

When it comes to the second P, **protect**, the male ego is heavily involved. When a man sees a woman for the first time, the need to protect may come shortly after the desire to pursue. It's an inborn reaction that is triggered the moment we begin caring about someone. Hell, sometimes it's triggered before we even realize that we care. The bottom line is, if you are a person of interest, don't be surprised if he starts sticking his neck out to protect you--and make sure you recognize what that means. Ladies, don't mistake his desire to step up and protect you as an infringement on your independence. His actions will speak far louder than his words, so let him be a man and show you how he feels about you.

The next P, **provide** is yet another instinct involving the male ego. This is where the male testosterone has kicked in and machismo is in full effect. Nothing makes a man feel better than providing for his family and loved ones. There is no greater sense of pride than making sure the family has what they need. We provide for those we love, honor, and respect. Providing for a woman during the dating stage is a sign that we care about their well-being. Although we respect an independent woman, we want to be sure that we can sustain, supplement or enhance her standard of living, rather than downgrade it. Getting up and going to work every day is a large part of our self-worth as men. A man's self-value is strongly based on how well we provide for our loved ones. Being unemployed or unable to provide a quality lifestyle for our household is a detriment to our manhood.

Ladies, be well aware of the man's need to provide while communicating, planning, and defining the roles in your relationship. Feel out the type of man you are dealing with. Will he be a provider or someone who plans to suck the life out of you? Figure out where his head is in the beginning to avoid the heartache later on.

The final P is the male's desire to **penetrate**, which shouldn't come as a surprise. It is well within a man's nature to desire penetration when he sees an attractive female who has it going on and possesses any other desirable traits. When there is a desire for sexual gratification, it is evident in nearly every one of his interactions, conversations, and deeds. It's at the forefront of his mind and will almost always arise when he is communicating with the person of interest. If he's smooth, he'll try his best to conceal it, but he can rarely fool his counterpart. Those pheromones are real, y'all.

When the man's primary goal is to penetrate, and the female wants more than that, it is important for the female to realize one thing. Image is everything! As I mentioned previously, how a woman presents herself will shape the direction of the relationship. She must hold off on indulging in sexual interactions with him for as long as she possibly can. Regardless of how much you are feeling him, you won't gain anything by giving in to his sexual desires right away. Some people believe that good sex makes a good relationship. I'm sorry to tell you...that ain't always true. I know we're in a new era where women feel like they don't have to wait, but if you want to be in a healthy, long-term relationship, you need to practice self-control. Odds are, he will not be contacting you for a second date if you give it up on the first night, unless he's looking for round two – **point blank period.**

If you're really vibing with him, spend ample time getting to know him and allowing him to know you. Differentiate yourself from all of the other women he has known by asking questions about what he likes to do, what his goals are, and what makes him happy. Trust me, in my experience, women who plan to give it up right away normally don't waste time asking those types of questions, or if she does, she isn't very interested in the answers.

Although a woman is placed in a category by a man, she does not have to stay there. It's essentially up to her to determine where she will fall in a man's life. If she has goals to sleep with him, this can easily happen. If she wants a long-term relationship with him and he sees her as a jump off, she has the power to change that as well. She can try to convince him otherwise, or she can simply walk away. The key to ensuring you are not placed in a category that disagrees with their relationship goals is to fight for what she expects and deserves. This includes communicating what her wants and needs are up front, sending the right signals, asking the right questions, and, no matter what, conducting herself with respect.

As you can see, there are some vast differences in how men and women think, which affects how we communicate. Understanding your counterpart's mindset will help you bridge the communication gap and connect with them on a deeper level. Keep in mind the differences in the way you think and communicate when choosing your words and interpreting their actions. It's best to remain objective, and most importantly, take notice of verbal and nonverbal cues in order to hear what is and is not being said.

TOPIC ELEVEN

Pre-Marital Counseling

Once you have reached the point in your relationship where you have openly committed to spending the rest of your lives together, it is important to adjust your communication methods accordingly. Planning to live, love, and act as one is the ultimate commitment and should be treated with the utmost respect. Before saying I do, you should pledge your time and efforts to finding out as much as you can about your partner and their goals for the life you will share together. I'm not suggesting that you grill them interrogation style, but you will need to actively converse about short and long-term goals, values, beliefs, and lifestyle choices. Relationships and marriages are like building a house. You need to consider who you're building with, where you would you like to be in the long-term before making the commitment, and what type of maintenance is needed to sustain your investment.

It is within premarital counseling that the mind shift happens. You go from dating to seriously thinking about building the rest of your life together. It's what I like to call the *forever mentality*. Entering into the next phase in your relationship can be exciting, magical, and scary. By adopting the forever mentality, you are able to look at the relationship from a brand new standpoint. Start studying your vows now and familiarize yourself with the words so you're not just reciting them on your big day. If you are already married, revisit those words and reflect on them. What do they mean to you now? How do they apply to your feelings for your partner and what you're building together?

Premarital counseling studies show decreases in divorce by fifty percent. Therefore, counseling with a pastor or therapist is highly recommended in order to make certain you are on the same path, or at least headed in the same direction. **In a successful marriage, outside factors are non-factors**. Being unified in your thinking and your plans to reach your collective goals is essential for longevity and happiness. You will have a life partner that will stand with you while you face the highest of highs and the lowest of lows. Counseling helps in setting the foundation that will support you in times of joy, pain and everything in between. Let's take a look at some of the topics you should be sure to discuss independently or bring up in your counseling sessions.

1. **Make sure you are equally yoked.** If you turned a blind eye to the fact that your partner is still in bed instead of meeting you for church service, you may want to rethink the impact it will have on your marriage. Habits will only change if the need to change is felt by you or your partner. When it comes to a healthy marriage, you will need to make sure that you are being fulfilled. If you are a Christian and your spouse is not, or vice versa, that is a topic that needs to be explored. Who will officiate the wedding? How will the difference impact your life together? Take the time to figure out how your belief differences will play out in your life together.

2. **Ask the things you would never ask before marriage.** Now is the time to get all up in their business. While dating, we tend to be on our best behavior. We don't want to rock the boat by asking intrusive questions that could offend or push our mate away. While this is understandable, once you have decided to spend the rest of your life together, this should no longer the case. Now that the commitment has been made, it's time to ask them about all of the things you have been wondering.

Questions about family history, genetic background, and physical and mental health predispositions are all fair game and are things you should know about your spouse. Set up an official time to discuss your concerns and remember to be tactful and respectful in your approach. No one likes to be railroaded.

3. **Discuss what-if scenarios for the sake of planning and discovering differences of opinion on important topics.** Think about your life together and what you want it to include. Would you like to purchase a home? Have children? Travel frequently? Invest? These goals all require strategic planning and being on one accord. In your discussions, be sure to outline your individual and collective expectations and figure out a way to compromise.

4. **Agree on a wedding budget and living arrangements.** Planning your wedding is one of the most exciting times in your relationship to date. Don't ruin it by bickering over how much money is being spent on the wedding dress, venue, and cake. Agree on how much you can afford to spend, then create a plan to contribute to the wedding fund to ensure the expenses are covered on time. You will also need to consider whose household you will move into if you are not already living together. Do you want to purchase a new home? If so, when? Plan out the details as soon as possible to discover what your future joint financial responsibilities will look like.

5. **Credit and financial history.** Whether you choose to have a joint bank account or keep them separate, you should discuss your financial status. If you're planning to pursue some of the long-term financial goals stated previously, your financial history and current standing will play significant roles in the process. If you are experiencing financial hardship or suspect your partner is, the time to discuss the details is now.

6. **Establish an intimacy and date night schedule.** You may not see the need for an intimacy or date night routine at this point in your relationship, but as the passion dies down, children come, or when any other life situations occur, you will find yourself in need of a schedule to make sure you are staying on

track romantically. Life happens and you can easily forget to put a date night on the calendar for the week or even the month. Make sure you're making your time together a priority in the midst of your everyday demands and activities.

Remember, money, sex, and kids are the topics couples argue most about. Be sure to address these topics on a regular basis with your partner, especially during your therapy sessions. When it comes to getting the most out of your therapy sessions, don't be ashamed to discuss intimate topics in front of your pastor or counselor. They have heard far more than you think and have successfully helped many couples with working through their issues. Leverage this resource to help you lay the groundwork you need for an abundant life together.

TOPIC TWELVE

Marriage Meetings

Your marriage can fulfill many significant needs in your life. Your spouse can be your lover, best friend, confidant, co-parent, your support system, and even your business partner. More ties with your spouse means more nurturing time will be required to ensure your relationship is healthy, happy, and running smoothly. Remember, your relationship is a journey, not a final destination. Relationships—especially marriages—require hard work, dedication, and patience; so it is important to focus on it regularly. Staying on track and delving deeper into the issues and matters that affect your rapport should be at the forefront of your collective relationship goals.

Remember, relationships are not 50/50. It's not enough to meet your partner halfway, because they may not always have the mental or emotional capacity to kick in the other half. Then the "what have you done for me lately" mode kicks in. Successful relationships require a 100/100 mentality. Be willing to go all the way and stand in the gap when your partner needs you to. In doing this, you have will have the *forever mentality* necessary to sustain your relationship over time.

We discussed the importance of temperature checks in Topic Eight. The next step is to conduct meetings at least twice a month to check the pulse of your marriage, keep your household running smoothly, discuss your goals for the current and upcoming year, finances, kids, and family vacations. Let's take a look at how bi-weekly meetings can develop and foster healthier communication skills and practices in your relationship.

MEETINGS FOR HOUSEHOLD OR PERSONAL ISSUES:

- **Provides a positive platform for each person's thoughts and input to be heard.** Each person should feel empowered to share their thoughts openly without the fear of judgment, being minimized, or being dismissed. These discussions should take place in a positive and healthy environment where communicating concerns and opinions regarding the relationship or household matters are openly encouraged.
- **Provides a platform to discuss issues affecting the household.** Each meeting's purpose is to provide a safe space for you to discuss topics that have a significant impact on your home and the best way to resolve them. Each person should attempt to contribute to the topic list and to the discussion. It's important to be contributory, not reactive.
- **Provides a platform for each person's thoughts and input to be heard.** Each person should have the opportunity to weigh in on the issue or topic and provide their input. One person should not dominate the conversation and each person should be encouraged to share their thoughts in order to reach a compromise and move forward with reaching an amicable solution.
- **Provides a platform to reach a solution to household or relationship issues.** After listening to one another and agreeing on the issues and observations at hand, each person should contribute to the process of resolving the issue. Action items should be agreed upon, designated, and followed up on during the next meeting.

PLANNING FOR UPCOMING EVENTS:

- **Provides a platform to discuss goals, dreams, and plans.** This is the ideal time to take a look at what you want to accomplish over the short and long-term. Vacations, investments, buying a home, and or home renovations all require active planning and financial commitment. Take the time to discuss what you want to happen and how you will get there as a team. Set dates, create a budget, discuss the details of your research and make a plan.

- **Update your calendar for the year and verbally commit to accomplishing your goals.** Take a look at the year, if you haven't already, and account for the monthly events you anticipate. Is there a milestone birthday coming up or an anniversary to celebrate? Do you plan to launch a new business together? How about adding onto the house? You may want to get some new patio furniture. Talk about your goals and begin the research and planning process to make it happen.

The meetings should be no more than 45 minutes and should be held in a quiet private place with no distractions. Try to aim for the same day and time of the week to create a habit. If you cannot have the meeting due to a scheduling conflict, always move the meeting to another day in the same week, being mindful not to allow more than 14 days between them. Keep a positive attitude and take notes between meetings to make sure all pertinent issues are discussed at length. Most importantly, stick with it. Within a couple months of having these meetings, you have my word that things will run a lot smoother in your household and in your relationship.

TOPIC THIRTEEN

Apologizing Like You Mean It

Conflict is inevitable in any relationship – particularly in long-term romantic relationships. We tend to forget that constructive conflict is actually a healthy component of any relationship. We are fully entitled to possess and experience our emotions, feelings, and beliefs. Consequently, receiving validation for our opinions is a critical part of communication and building solid, long-lasting relationships. When a difference of opinion leads to forms of unhealthy communication and prolonged conflict, we have to take a look at the part we played in the situation and take ownership of any undesired outcomes. We also need to examine our intentions to determine if an apology on our part is needed.

So, for example, if you and your partner are no longer on speaking terms or have butted heads about a particular situation, you should ask yourself three questions:

***

STEP ONE: SELF-EXAMINATION

1.) Was my overall intention pure?
2.) Was my delivery positive?
3.) Did my words and actions create the positive impact I desired?

The questions may seem repetitive at first, but take a closer look at each one. You might have had good intentions when you first entered the conversation, but the dynamics could have easily changed at some point. Maybe your partner said something you didn't like, or you felt your point wasn't getting across, so you felt the need to spell it out for them. You could have attempted to be positive in your delivery, but your impact may have come off as condescending, rude, insensitive, or judgmental. Your intention may have been impure to start with, which, consequently, impacts everything that comes out of your mouth in a negative manner. However it goes, self-examination and diplomacy are needed to get to the root of the issue. If, for whatever reason, you find fault on your part in the outcome, you should take fully ownership and accountability.

***

STEP TWO: DISCOVERY AND REFLECTION

You may not have a full understanding of the effect your words and actions had on your partner yet. Sure, you can reflect on the details of your interactions, speculate, and attempt to resolve things on your own, but there is only one way to get a more accurate understanding of what actually transpired. You need to speak to your partner to get their point of view. You need to ask them to explain their version of what transpired, how they felt during the situation, and their conclusion. In doing so, you will have a better idea of what occurred and how the interaction made them feel. In doing so, the missing pieces will eventually become clear. You may not see eye-to-eye on everything and your perceptions will likely differ. But if you are truly invested in finding a resolution, you must consult your partner before moving forward.

You will want to ask questions to gain more information from your mate to see if any emotional damage or hurt was caused. Sincerity is needed to preserve the relationship and to move forward in the resolution process. Here are a few tips on how to go about it:

1.) **Find time to speak face-to-face.** Do not attempt to have this conversation over the phone, text, email, or via direct messaging. Sit down with your partner in a quiet, private place where you can speak uninterrupted.

2.) **Be sincere.** Inquire about their true feelings and opinions about what occurred.

3.) **Be curious.** Ask for their point of view and do not interrupt them. Allow them to express all of their thoughts and work through their issues verbally.

4.) **Listen actively.** Do not think about your response while they are talking. Really listen to what they have to say and provide non-verbal cues that you're listening, such as head nods and direct eye contact.

5.) **Clarify.** Ask follow-up questions to get more information instead of making assumptions.

6.) **Be patient.** Do not rush the process. Simply listen to gain an understanding, not to formulate an argument.

7.) **Gain a thorough understanding.** Don't move on in the discussion until you learn why your partner is upset. Furthermore, don't ever assume you know exactly how your partner is feeling. You never will. You are not them. But you can still express empathy by trying your best to understand. Ask if you have done something wrong and get the specific details.

8.) **Let it marinate.** Take some time to process all of the new information before moving forward with asking for or giving an apology. There is nothing worse than spilling your heart out to someone only to learn they didn't listen to a word you said. The only thing that comes close is an insincere, rushed, knee-jerk apology: *"Oh, I did that? My bad...you forgive me?"* Work through it–sleep on it if you have to–then revisit it.

9.) **Know your role before asking for or giving an apology.** You should be informed about what you contributed to the undesired outcome. Whether it was your tone, your attitude, an assumption that you made, or nothing at all, you should have the confidence to stand in your truth. No soap boxes, please, just the confidence to determine what's right and wrong in the scenario. If you determine you have done something to hurt your partner, you will need to start thinking about how to give a sincere apology.

✳✳✳

STEP THREE: TAKING OWNERSHIP

Once you take the time to consider your partner's stance in your disagreement, your perspective should change. It may not change by 180 degrees, but it should certainly shift to some degree. If not, you will need to reevaluate your listening skills and your ability to reason and empathize. After you have reflected on your opinions as well as your partner's take on what occurred, you may conclude that you have had some level of fault in the undesired outcome.

The next thing to consider is whether or not you are ready to own your contribution to the problem. No matter how big or small of a part you played, if you have some role in the outcome, you will need to take some degree of accountability. This will be needed if you are authentic in your desire to move toward a resolution with your mate. You will need to ask yourself, if it is better to be right or to be happy. Is resolving the issue truly your agenda? I'm not urging you to take the blame for things you have not done, as that can be viewed by your partner as being condescending or dismissive. But, right or wrong, you can still be the bigger person and initiate the process of moving toward a solution together. Sometimes it may come down to agreeing to disagree and letting bygones be bygones.

***

STEP FOUR: THE APOLOGY

Now, let's talk about how *not* to go about giving a sincere apology. You will want to avoid issuing conditional apologies such as:

> *"I'm sorry if you felt..."*
>
> *"I'm sorry, but..."*
>
> *"[Insert what you think they want to hear here]."*

"I'm sorry *if* you felt..." This is an example of a conditional apology. The "if" changes the whole context of the statement and cancels out the impact of the intended apology. Inserting the "if" means the speaker is simply guessing the reason why the person they are apologizing to is upset. The speaker hasn't taken the time to uncover what the person is upset about and is certainly not acknowledging their own part in the problem.

"I'm sorry, *but...*" This is another example of negating the apology with one simple word. "But" has no place in a sincere apology. The word "but" shifts the accountability from the speaker onto someone or something else. The speaker does not acknowledge their reason for apologizing in this example, making the attempt hollow and meaningless.

"[Insert what you think they want to hear here]." Apologizing purely for the sake of dismissing your partner's feelings, thoughts or opinions, in an effort to move on or to take the heat off of yourself is unproductive and ineffective. This way of thinking is unhealthy and can offend, anger, or disappoint your partner because they may feel as though you are trying to sweep the issue and their feelings beneath the rug. If you don't want to apologize, then don't. But don't insult your loved one by dismissing them or their feelings.

Now let's take a closer look at what you *should* remember when apologizing to your loved one. The key characteristics you should possess when approaching your partner is modesty, sincerity, repentance, and accountability.

THE FOUR-PART APOLOGY

1.) "I'm sorry for…"
2.) "It was wrong because…"
3.) "In the future, I will…"
4.) "Will you forgive me?"

The first step is the ownership of what the speaker did wrong. It's a simple statement with no if's or but's about it.

"I'm sorry for withdrawing a large sum of money from our savings account without speaking with you about it first."

The second step is the speaker's acknowledgment of what was wrong about their actions, words, or reaction. It validates the other person's feelings and shows that the speaker is fully aware of the transgression.

"It was wrong of me to withdraw the money. I know we had an agreement that we would make each other aware of our financial transactions. I realize that I violated your trust by doing so."

The third step explains what the speaker has learned about the impact of their actions, words, or reaction on their partner and how they plan to correct it moving forward.

"In the future, I will be sure to let you know before I withdraw funds from the account of over two hundred dollars."

The final step formally asks for acceptance from your partner. It can be the hardest part of the apology because many of us don't deal well with being at the mercy of others. We are looking at the possibility of rejection–or, depending on how critical the mistake was, the end of the relationship–which can be challenging. But this step demonstrates to your partner that you are not only willing to own your part in the problem, but you are also actively seeking their approval and acceptance. This speaks volumes to your sincerity and intent.

"Once again, I apologize. Can you forgive me or do you need more time to think it over?"

Apologizing–whether you feel you are right or wrong–can be one of the hardest parts of your relationship, but it can also be the most necessary. Gaining a full understanding of the importance of a sincere apology is not only essential for effective communication, but it is the best way to showcase your commitment to the elevation of your relationship. Remember, it's not about how you are tested, but how you endure and prevail.

SECTION II: LEVELING UP: DEEPENING THE TRUST

Trust is just a five-letter word, but it has such powerful meaning and implication. Just speaking this word can evoke a wide range of emotions, personal experiences, and feelings. The impact alone can make most people cringe.

Leveling up is a practice that should be exercised after every failed relationship. This is an opportunity to examine where you went wrong and to reset your boundaries and expectations. It is a time to decide what your standards are what you your relationships will look like moving forward.

When thinking of all the times you've placed your trust in someone, told them your darkest secrets, shared your dinner table with them, and had pillow talk with them only to have them crush you with betrayal, it stirs something up deep inside. When trust is broken verbally, through infidelity, or unintentionally, it may make you wonder if that person ever knew the full value of your trust. Did they even know what it really meant to you or to them?

So many of us have been deceived, hurt, and broken because we gave too much of ourselves, invited someone in too quickly, were too accommodating, too believing, too desperate or lonely, or lacked to see the value within ourselves to use proper discernment.

Now, let's take time to examine all of the elements of our relationships that are developed, exposed, and explored because of trust.

TOPIC FOURTEEN

Forgiveness

Now that we have discussed the components of an authentic apology, the next topic we will cover is forgiveness. When a situation affects your relationship and calls for forgiveness—and the situation will arise—in your relationship, you should treat it with the respect and seriousness it deserves. Forgiveness is one of the main components of a healthy functional relationship and it requires a great deal of trust. You don't necessarily have to regain 100% of your trust in your partner to forgive, but you will need trust for what comes next. You or your partner must feel like there is a strong chance that the offense won't happen again in order to move forward in the relationship after forgiveness.

Learning to forgive your partner is critical for the sake of healing, rebuilding trust, and maintaining a healthy relationship. Forgiveness is also essential for personal and collective growth. When you do not forgive the person who has hurt you, you will find yourself experiencing resentment, disdain, and prolonged pain. Progression and evolution within a relationship is not possible with forgiveness.

When you forgive others, you are able to gain clarity on what has happened, how it made you feel, and what you will and will not accept in the future. However, let me be clear on one thing. There is a big difference between accepting your partner for who they are and outright accepting abuse from them.

Forgiveness is not designed to excuse or ignore poor behavior, abuse, or any other unhealthy patterns or behaviors in your relationship. Forgiveness also does not mean that you condone the action(s) that hurt you. Forgiveness is for your own healing, growth and peace of mind, not for your partner. So, if you have a partner who is mentally, emotionally, or physically abusive, unfaithful, disrespectful, or who is not adding value to your life, my advice will always be to leave that situation as soon as you can.

If you or your partner has made a mistake that requires forgiveness, there should be a mutual understanding that forgiveness is a process. The rate of forgiveness has many variables, so it would be unreasonable to assume that there is a one size fits all timeframe for how long it takes someone to forgive. How long it takes a person to forgive depends on the individual's emotional state and how deeply they were impacted, it also depends on the sincerity of the offending party, the severity of the transgression, and how the information was discovered or received.

Forgiveness is often a complicated process and the timeframe can vary, based on the severity of the following elements:

- Resentment
- Distrust
- Betrayal
- Disappointment
- Pain
- Anger
- Vulnerability
- Unhealthy patterns or cycles

The individual's emotional state. If you have been wronged or have wronged someone, the next steps after the apology is given are often unclear. It heavily depends on where the person is mentally at the time. They can feel some or all of the emotions stated above. For example, if there were already doubts about something happening and they are confirmed, the person may be hesitant to let go of their resentment because they feel they are letting you get away with it. They may become distant and cold with you because they feel violated.

How deeply the offended party was impacted. If a significant emotional impact has been made, someone may be slower to forgive than they would for a lesser violation. They may need to take some time to process your apology, what has happened and what their next steps should be. The ball is in their court to decide whether they want to stay in the relationship. Pressuring someone to decide before they have had enough time think about things only makes things worse. Make sure to give or take the time you need so that the issue can be addressed, ironed out, and put behind you.

The sincerity of the offending party. How the apology is delivered and what is said speaks large volumes. If there is sincerity, compassion, and authenticity in the words that are said, it increases the odds that they will be received in a more objective way. Now, don't get me wrong, there are some situations that you just can't apologize or buy your way out of. But if there is remorse and acknowledgment of wrongdoing, the odds of a positive impact on the outcome are greater.

The severity of the transgression. How bad was it…really? Dishonesty? Infidelity? Betrayal? The severity of the action will directly impact the length of time it will take you or your partner to forgive. The further the setback, the longer the journey back to normalcy. Be cognizant of that and give yourself or your partner the time they need to debrief on it all.

How was the information discovered or received? Was the offender forthcoming right after it happened? Was there lying involved to cover up the details? Did the offended have to find out on their own? The level of damage to the trust and faith in the relationship depends heavily on this.

Deal breaker? In the first topic, we discussed setting the proper expectations for yourself before entering a relationship and communicating that to your partner upfront. We defined deal breakers as qualities, characteristics, or circumstances that you're not willing to compromise on. We also discussed refusing to give up on your standards. Ask yourself if the action was one of those things you were not willing to compromise on at the beginning of the relationship. If you are the offender, ask yourself the same. Do you really want them to be responsible for them having to go back on their principles because you couldn't respect their boundaries?

After reviewing this information and making the choice to forgive, the first question the offended party must ask is if it is worth staying in the relationship. As I mentioned previously, forgiving someone does not mean that you are excusing or ignoring their behavior. You still have the ability to walk away from the relationship if you feel it is harmful to your well-being. You do not owe your partner anything if you feel as though you are not valued or respected in your relationship. But you **do** owe them the courtesy of letting your issues with them go or seeking therapy if you choose to stay and work things out, if needed.

Here are a few destructive behaviors you should avoid when struggling to forgive your partner:

- Vindictiveness
- Pettiness
- Picking fights
- Holding it over their head
- Holding a grudge
- Constantly bringing it up
- Remaining distant
- Painting an immoral picture of them
- Being accusatory
- Being paranoid or overly insecure

You'll know when you have been forgiven or have truly forgiven someone when the relationship shows continual progress in the right

78

direction. The state of your relationship will not be restored immediately, but it will improve over time, if effort is made on both ends. The trust will be rebuilt and the foundation of the relationship will be regenerated over time. You're on the right path. Just hang in there, family!

TOPIC FIFTEEN

Ensuring Privacy in Your Relationship

Healthy relationships thrive on mutual respect, love, communication, trust, and **loyalty**! Loyalty is everything in a relationship and it is tested on a regular basis by those who are outside of your relationship. People would be lying if they didn't admit they may be curious about the intimate details of any particular relationship. It's human nature to wonder about what happens behind the closed doors of others. But curiosity is where it should end. Discussing the intimate details of your relationship with anyone other than your partner is unhealthy behavior. Everyone else should be on the *outside* looking *in*. When you are with someone you love and they share private things with you, you should feel privileged to know this information about them. They trust you enough to open up to you and that's what makes your relationship special. No one else deserves to know the details about their private life, opinions, or circumstances.

WHAT TO KEEP PRIVATE IN YOUR RELATIONSHIP

1. **All things sexual.** Bedroom behavior should remain there. Any details about what happens there—especially male endowment, performance issues, how frequently you have intercourse, and infidelity—should be kept between you two.

2. **Any arguments you have and their detail.** Refrain from sharing with others that you are not speaking to, are frustrated with, or are mad at your partner. The only person you should be discussing that with is your partner.

3. **Your finances.** If you and your partner are experiencing financial trouble or if you are doing well financially, it's best to keep those details to yourself. One is private and the other can be perceived as boasting.

4. **Your relationship arrangements.** It's none of your friends' business if you have an open relationship with your partner or if you're swingers. This is just bedroom talk extended. Keep it private.

5. **All pillow talk topics.** This includes innermost secrets and fears, details about their childhood, family, or details about their close friends, insecurities, and areas of vulnerability. Discussing any of this with someone else without your partner's consent is a gross violation of their trust. And it's just plain wrong.

6. **Household occurrences.** Anything that goes on in your house of a private matter should not be discussed with anyone outside of your relationship. This could include issues between your partner and your child, your beef with his family, baby's mama or daddy, etc. Family difficulties are a matter of privacy.

7. **Your partner's flaws or shortcomings.** It may seem harmless to make light of your partner's inability to master a skill, or their struggles with different things, but that is not a healthy way to represent your relationship to others. It's important to paint your partner in a positive light. You never know when they will need to come around your loved ones and you don't want them to feel uncomfortable.

8. **Anything that you wouldn't say with them standing beside you.** No explanation needed.

I know this list seems like common sense, but it happens a lot more often than you think. I'm sure you are, or have been, guilty of several of these habits in the past. Discussing private relationship issues with people outside of your relationship breaches the that confidence your partner has in you and will likely cause problems later on down the line. If you have any hesitation about sharing something about your relationship or your partner with someone else, don't.

TOPIC SIXTEEN

Handling Finances

Money matters are the second leading cause of marital problems and divorce. Given the fact that financial issues are only second to infidelity, I'd say we should definitely take a closer look at the ways they can impact your relationship.

When it comes to handling finances, it's important to recognize the weight it holds in your relationship before taking it to the next level. An estimated forty percent of divorced couples note finance-related issues as their reason for calling it quits. Just think about it: we spend most of our adult lives working to earn money in order to provide for ourselves and our families, so making decisions that impact someone else's finances is a delicate position to be in. Engaging in open and healthy communication that is centered on trust is the biggest factor in establishing a collaborative and lucrative partnership regarding your collective finances. When tough decisions call for immediate action, having a solid foundation in place is critical in making sure that both parties have each other's best interests at heart.

Financial expert Christina Grice, founder of Life in Balance LLC advises, "Before you and your partner can even consider devising a financial plan together, you must be prepared to put everything out in the open and address it impartially. Level up knowing that you are building a stronger, more prosperous foundation together. Avoid sitting in past events and using them to harbor resentment and anger. Start fresh. Be forgiving and think wisely. Remember one of the most difficult things is to be vulnerable without assurance, so give each other grace."

SIX STEPS TO CREATING A SOLID FINANCIAL FOUNDATION

We place the majority of our security in our finances. A sense of financial security shapes our future and helps us prepare for the unknown. Every day, life shows us how fragile we really are and that preparation is the only true way to ensure we will have a net in place to catch us when life knocks us down. So what happens when you enter a relationship with someone else and choose to combine your assets? What if their way of handling finances differs slightly, or even drastically from yours? How will this transition shift the dynamics of your relationship?

LET'S TALK ABOUT IT.

There are quite a few ways to address money while in a committed relationship and I'm not here to judge or tell you how you should do that. My goal is to help you create a platform that enables you to discuss your financial goals with your significant other and to prevent future static that may arise due to differences in your money management practices.

Step One: Discover your partner's money mindset. As I mentioned previously, we work hard for our money. So when it comes down to choosing how to spend it, your opinions may differ from your mate's. The main reason is, we all have different relationships with money. We were raised with separate sets of parents who had their own unique financial experiences. Of course, you can't expect your spending habits and financial values to mirror your partner's, but there should be a mutual respect for varying opinions on how the money is spent. So take the time to talk about it. Be honest, hear them, out, ask questions, and figure out how you can handle the household finances in a way that it is comfortable for each of you. Your plan should include a set of short and long-term goals as well as collective ones.

Step Two: Learn About Your Partner's Financial History & Goals. In Topic Eleven, I mentioned it was important to familiarize yourself with your partner's credit and financial history and to disclose your own economic status to discover your collective monetary mindset. Ideally, this is accomplished before taking your relationship to the next level.

In order to determine how the household finances will be handled, you will first need to discuss your financial goals. These are the monetary goals you would like to accomplish outside of routine bill paying and savings habits. Would you like to be debt free in five years, invest in real estate or mutual funds, start a business, or maybe relocate? Discovering your partner's goals creates the opportunity to create a plan that incorporates your collective ideas.

Step Three: Sum up and Address Debt. The next step is to address the elephant in the room: pre-existing debt. Now that you're married or in a committed relationship and living together, it's time to consider how you will handle addressing the debt that was accumulated on each end before you got to this point. Failing to have this conversation, as awkward as it can be, can lead to major misconceptions later that can impact each of you in a negative way. If you beg to differ, just think about how low credit scores and garnished paychecks will affect the money that is coming into your home for paying bills. Discuss your debt in-depth and form a plan to raise your credit scores and eventually become debt-free. It doesn't happen overnight, but if we fail to plan, we plan to fail.

Step Four: Create an Initial Budget. Now that you've gotten the formalities out the way, it's time to create a budget that you will both adhere to. It would benefit you to avoid starting off with an elaborate budget that will be difficult to get your head around. You can begin by listing fundamental elements such as the shared household bills and responsibilities, creating a plan to contribute to a three to six-month's income reserve for emergencies, and plan for future expenses, trips, and household projects. Remember, the budget can be customized to include your financial goals as they change over time.

Step Five: Devise a Money Allocation Plan. Now let's take a look at handling your bank accounts. You will need to agree on how to pay the bills and manage the finances. Opening a joint bank account is a common practice for couples with shared financial responsibilities because it simplifies the bill payment, budgeting, and spending analysis processes. If you struggle with the idea of all of your money being funneled into one pot, consider keeping the joint account for household-related expenses and maintaining your separate bank accounts for all of your personal spending. This will eliminate potential arguments regarding private spending habits. Be advised that you will need to determine together what qualifies for a household expense and what is personal. For example, should trips to the hair salon and barber shop be deducted from the joint account? What about gas and eating out for lunch during the week? Bring it all up beforehand and discuss these things regularly to ensure you're on the same page.

Step Six: Address long-term investments, accounts and financial arrangements. In addition, there are many other things to discuss, such as keeping your life insurance policies up to date, managing your investments, and how much to contribute to your retirement accounts. Remember to discuss the touchy areas like how inheritances will be spent if one of you is a beneficiary for a parent's life insurance policy. It may be a ways off, but it's never too soon to discuss those things. By having these discussions, you put yourselves in a position to have one less thing to think about it when that unfortunate event comes.

Shining a light on how you will approach your finances on a unified front will benefit your relationship, but it will also create honesty and transparency in the way you communicate with one another. The added bonus is building the type of trust that will sustain your union for years to come.

TOPIC SEVENTEEN

Is It Cool to Have Mad Money?

Growing up, I would often overhear the term "Mad Money" sporadically mentioned in adult conversations. The term was interesting and unique to me, so each time it was spoken, it always caught my attention. I would hear comments like, "Girl, you better have that mad money–just in case he starts acting a fool." My young mind wondered what the meaning was behind those words. What was mad money and why would a woman need something like that on reserve? As I grew older and gained a better understanding of the complexities of relationships, I learned exactly what mad money was. As a man, I had to come to terms with my opinions on this practice and how it would potentially affect my future relationships.

For those of you who aren't familiar with the term mad money, it is a financial stash that a person–in most cases, a woman–reserves in case of an emergency. Most often, they are liquid assets like on-hand cash or a separate savings account, but it can also be short-term investments. The existence of the account or stash may be private or known to the other party in the relationship. The main purpose of the money is to serve as a nest egg to be used as a "plan B" financial option when the saver finds his or herself in a situation having to make a hasty purchase or retreat from an unfortunate situation or circumstance involving their significant other. The amount of money in the account or stash can vary, based on the purpose it serves. It could be enough money for a bus or plane ticket, first and last month's rent, or even tens of thousands of dollars.

As I mentioned previously, the person's mate may or may not be aware of the money, which leads us to the point of this topic. Is having mad money cool? Should a person have separate money reserved solely for the purpose of making a major independent decision that affects the status of the relationship? Is the money's existence ethical and constructive while in a committed relationship? Is the owner of the money considering how their choice to have this money impacts the other party in the relationship? Should the owner's loyalty to the relationship and commitment be questioned by their partner because of their need to have the money reserved? So many questions, right? My bad, that's the radio show host in me.

Let's take a look at some of the positive and negative impacts mad money can potentially have on relationships.

Pros:

- Fosters a sense of independence
- Funds can be used in case of emergency for both parties
- Creates financial security for the entire household

Cons:

- Funds can be used as an exit strategy in your relationship hastily and without proper reflection
- Other person may view funds as a crutch/safety net and makes bad choices on their part
- May create a threat in other person's mind about the account owner's commitment to the relationship

Here are my thoughts on the subject. I, personally, don't like to use the term mad money. I prefer to think of that pool of money as a necessity for each person in the relationship. Having your own assets on hand can be beneficial to both parties. The reality is **no** relationship, no matter the level of commitment, is guaranteed to last. Having your own money that is separate from your partner's is no different than having a pre-nuptial agreement in place at the beginning of your marriage. As we stated previously, the number one reason for divorce is financial-affiliated issues. You cannot afford the risk involved with not having a financial safe haven prepared. You can view your financial reserve the same as having a life insurance policy set up. At the time you pass away, you need to be assured that your spouse and loved ones are taken care of. But the primary goal is to assure that your loved ones are not burdened with the financial responsibility of burying you. Yes, they may have access to the money in your account to do so, but it's not good to assume that they will. Yes, you may be working every day and be in a good financial position, but that may not be the case when you've had enough and are ready to go.

So, should you have mad money? My answer would be no. There is no reason for secrecy when it comes to finances in a relationship. Where there is secrecy, there is an opportunity for distrust. In my opinion, if there are separate accounts, there should be a clear understanding of their existence and the intent for the use of said accounts.

Mad money should not be viewed as an "easy out" for your relationship. I strongly suggest taking the time to think things through before leaving your relationship. Avoid making hasty decisions. Although the decision to stay or leave is ultimately yours, consider including your mate in the decision-making process for your own closure and theirs.

SECTION III: ONGOING SUPPORT AND RELATIONSHIP MAINTENANCE

It is vital that you care about your mate's happiness and what is important to them. This component of maintaining the health of your relationship cannot be overlooked. Knowing your partner's needs, becoming familiar with their patterns, and being in tune with them are parts of providing them with the support they require to be happy and fulfilled.

Focus on rekindling the romance and showing appreciation for your partner. Revisit fond memories, appreciate the simple things and spark a conversation on how far you've come together. Lastly, self-care is a great way to invest in yourself as well as the health of your relationship. Burnout can be a real danger to the growth of relationship and can be easily avoided.

Let's find out how implementing these elements can help you level up in your relationship.

TOPIC EIGHTEEN

Knowing Your Partner's Needs

The truth is, we are most aware of our needs when they aren't being met. This is when we become hyperaware of how the failure of our partner to acknowledge our needs impacts us. It's safe to say that we all have unique desires that critically impact our behavior and interactions within our relationships. Taking the time to familiarize yourself with your partner's needs is not only an expression of your love and commitment, but it is a significant investment in the well-being of our relationship.

You are not a mind reader and never will be, which is why it is critical that you and your partner understand that becoming familiar with each other's needs will not happen overnight. To get there requires persistence and patience, which are paramount to you learning what is best for your partner's overall wellbeing. Your desire to see them happy, thriving, and doing well for themselves will inspire your everyday efforts to discover more about what they need from you to support their contentment.

The range of human needs is wide and deep, and each relationship is different because the individuals within it are different. This leaves us with an infinite mixture of needs that can develop and change in cycles and spurts over the course of a relationship. Abraham Maslow's hierarchy of needs, which is pictured below, categorizes the basic human needs in the base of the pyramid and the complexities increase as the pyramid peaks.

BASIC NEEDS WITHIN A RELATIONSHIP

Common needs within a relationship include: sexual intimacy, a sense of security, emotional connectedness and mental stability, appreciation, respect, and a sense of self-worth and perceived value.

The Sexual Need and Desire for Intimacy. This need is at the base of the pyramid and is often considered basic, due to its physiological affiliation. It is important to treat it as such. When your partner is sexually frustrated and in need of physical release, their body language tends to tell it all. We usually display telltale signs when our bodies have pent up stress and other emotions that can be easily soothed by sexual relief. Do her shoulders stiffen up? Does he have a certain gait in his walk? Do their eyes hold a certain look? Or are they simply on edge?

Whatever the case, once you determine your partner's silent cues when they are in need of sexual fulfillment, they become easier to recognize in the future. When that time comes, my advice is to get on it right away. You could have just had sex the previous night or even an hour prior—sometimes there is a need to turn up the physical contact in order to provide the necessary support to work through their situation.

Address their needs promptly and try not to let them leave the house in that state. Horniness can cloud a person's judgment drastically while in a stressful situation.

When it comes to intimacy, I think of women. This does not mean that men don't enjoy the intimate moments, but affection is most commonly associated with female needs. Women tend to enjoy being touched in a non-sexual way more often than men, such as hand holding, hugging, and being held and caressed. They enjoy romantic gestures like thoughtful gifts, date nights, and receiving cards and flowers at work. This intentional form of connection fulfills an emotional need for women. So, waiting until a birthday, anniversary, or monumental screw up to do these things will not be frequent enough. The "just because" flowers, texts, and gifts have the greatest impact because it's a spontaneous display of affection with no agenda involved. They like to know that they're in your thoughts when they are not with you.

When it comes to the fellas, a good home-cooked meal, a relaxing massage, keeping your physical appearance up, or new lingerie lets us know you've been thinking of us and our most basic needs.

The Need for a Sense of Security. The need for safety is the next level on the Maslow's hierarchy. This basic need applies to your relationship as well. There is nothing like feeling secure while with your partner. It eliminates stress and leaves more time for bonding and connecting on a higher level. Recognizing when your partner's sense of physical security is off is critical. Recognizing your partner's level of security regarding the status of your relationship is equally important. When your partner is feeling insecure about your level of commitment, faithfulness, and overall feelings about them, it shifts the dynamic of your relationship. There is no room for growth when doubt and fear exist. Be aware of their words and behaviors to gauge their level of trust they have in you and in your future together.

For example, if you notice your partner is double-checking everything you tell them and asking a multitude of questions regarding your whereabouts and motives, it's time to step in and reassure them.

Sometimes this happens because there has been infidelity in their past or in your current relationship. Sometimes it sprouts from your partner's own insecurities and/or lack of self-esteem. Whichever the case, you will both benefit greatly from addressing that need—immediately. Be mindful that your partner won't always be upfront about this need because they may feel as if it makes them appear weak or unstable. It is going to take some dedication on your part to make sure you are on the same page and that he or she knows that they have no reason to feel insecure about your relationship. Find out what makes them feel secure, whether it's public displays of affection, public acknowledgment in front of others or on social media, quality time, and transparency. Once you discover the solution, keep it in your back pocket, but be sure to use it sparingly to make sure it comes off as authentic to your partner and others.

The Need for Emotional Connectedness and Mental Stability. One of the most important elements of a relationship is to feel connected to your significant other. The emotional connections shared within an intimate relationship are unparalleled. Knowing that there is at least one person in this world who loves you, understands you, and is purposefully in your life is a wonderful feeling. In this form of connection, we find stability, trust, and compassion. Whenever that feeling is not deemed as reciprocated or justified, doubt creeps in.

We all have our ups and downs and whatever discord you are feeling toward your partner in any given moment should be worked through in a healthy manner. If you do not feel connected to them due to something they have said or done, be honest about it. Let them know about the effect of their actions and why you feel the way you do. Let them know if you need space and time to work through your feelings. But avoid punishing them. Giving them the silent treatment, leaving for an extended period of time with no contact, or taking your emotions out on them in a negative way will only create further distance and confusion between the two of you. When you notice that your partner may be feeling isolated from you, explain to them that you are taking the time you need to process your thoughts. If you don't plan to leave the relationship, let them know instead of trying to make them think they are losing you. If you are considering leaving the relationship, you should definitely let them know. It's better that they know what the possible ramifications of their actions are ahead of time.

If your partner has a need to feel connected to you and you are going through something that does not involve them, it's still okay to take some time. Just realize that they have needs as well. Inform them that you need time to work through your situation and that your current mood is not because a result of anything they have done. Then, either take your time and return to them ready to discuss whatever is bothering you or move on.

But don't leave them hanging while you're figuring things out. Codependency is never a healthy situation. If you find that your partner is too dependent on you for their own happiness and fulfillment and you find it draining, you may want to revisit whether that's something you can continue to tolerate for a long period of time. If it's not, I recommend having a conversation about it and seeking help right away.

It is also important to know your partner well enough to notice if they are on the verge of a breakdown. We all handle stress differently and your partner may not process it the same way as you. Be invested enough in their wellbeing to tune into them so that you can notice when they are at their breaking point. Then be prepared to step in and reroute them so that they can restore their mental health.

The Need to Feel Appreciated. This is an emotional need that can bear the most weight on your relationship when it is scarce or perceived as a missing component. There are many simple ways to reinforce your appreciation for your partner. Displaying gratefulness for what your partner symbolizes in your relationship and what they do for you, offering acknowledgment that shows them they are loved, and making a solid effort to establish and maintain an emotional connection take little effort and focus on the value your partner brings to the relationship. When we don't receive the consistent or even occasional positive feedback or praise for our efforts, it's natural to feel inadequate, unappreciated, or unimportant. In some cases, a person may feel that they aren't being seen or heard, and that they are being taken advantage of.

When you sense that your partner is beginning to feel unappreciated, don't rush in with compliments and praise right away. They will probably refuse to accept them at that point, due to their perceived insincerity on your part. They may feel as though you should have been thanking them all along and now you're choosing to overwhelm them with praise to make up for past neglect. When making an effort to show your partner how much you love and care about them in this context, remember that their rejection is rarely personal. It's most often related to internal issues they are struggling with. They may feel overlooked or neglected. They may think you're paying lip service in order to get something from them. But remain focused on your goal. Instead of giving up altogether, back up your compliment with valid reasons and examples. The more effort you make on your end, the more likely your partner will begin to put their guard down.

Make a vow to yourself to work through the hurt to get to the bottom line: making sure your partner feels valued and appreciated at all times. Make sure your compliments are occasional, but specific. Mention how great dinner was, how nice the lawn looks, or how good it feels to walk out and get into to a clean car. Send a text, write a note, or give them a hug and a long kiss. These small gestures can go a very long way in keeping the emotional connection between you and your partner strong, which only strengthens your relationship.

The Need to Feel Respected. This one is self-explanatory. There are countless ways we can cross the line of respect in our relationships daily. When you go from acting only on behalf of yourself to every move you make being measured against your relationship status and how you feel about your partner, things can get hairy. But the facts remain that while in a committed relationship, your main concern should be your partner's comfort level and whether they feel they have your respect at all times. This especially applies to how those outside of your relationship view your respect level.

I know you're thinking about my previous statement: *In a*

successful marriage, outside factors are non-factors. That still rings true. But that does not change the fact that the perception of others may still have a significant impact on the health of a relationship. To some degree, we do care about how others identify us and what they say about us. That's just human nature. Ways you can make sure your partner knows you have their back are: behaving like a person who's involved in a relationship in your partner's absence and presence, making sure your partner knows you can be trusted and that you would never do anything to hurt them, being honest and transparent with them. If you do these things, your partner will know they have your respect.

The Need to Feel a Sense of Self-Worth and Perceived Value. As previously mentioned, positive recognition from your partner satisfies a basic and critical need. It also contributes to your own self-worth and the sense of value you contribute to the relationship. Each of you play different roles, which means both parties need to have and demonstrate a positive self-image to feel a sense of belonging and purpose. Otherwise, what are you in the relationship for?

This is why a committed effort to building each other up and noticing the ebbs and flows and ups and downs within the relationship is critical. When you or your partner feel undervalued in the relationship, it may be time to revisit where the relationship is going. Have your collective goals and interests changed? Have your individual needs shifted? Is the passion still there? Regular check-ins ensure that each person feels as though the relationship is still headed in the right direction. This mutually-beneficial practice will prolong the relationship and create a positive platform for addressing future needs and concerns.

When we make sure our partner's needs are at the forefront of the relationship, we can't fail. The key is to commit to making sure they always know they're loved, appreciated and respected and then the rest will automatically follow.

TOPIC NINETEEN

Rekindling the Romance and Appreciation

It's time to be honest with yourself. As your relationships progresses, you should be proud of where you are, but you should also look at what got you to this point. If you have been with your partner for a while and have noticed that the thrill is gone, you need to start asking yourself some questions. Are you still doing what it took to get your partner to fall in love with you each day? The flirting? The lovey-dovey texts? The passionate lovemaking?

Are you still dating your partner?

I believe we've all been guilty of falling off with our romantic efforts at one point or another, so if that's the case with you, there's no judgment here at all. As a matter of fact, I'm here to offer some easy tips for getting back on track so you can rekindle the romance and sense of appreciation in your relationship.

First, we need to think about the reasons why this type of shift may have happened. Research has found it's actually pretty common to notice a decline in the level of romantic intensity in your relationship after the first two years. Passionate love has an expiration date for most relationships, and in most cases, it's due to a lack of curiosity. Plain and simple. In the beginning, we are so eager to learn more about this interesting individual that we barely let anything about this person affect us. We're much more willing to look past the little things–in fact, we find their small flaws fascinating. "Wow, they have so much character," we think. Then we find it less and less intriguing until that same "character trait" is irking the hell out of us a few years later.

So what exactly is passionate love and how do we prevent it from fading in our relationship? It all boils down to raw curiosity, compassion, and consistency. You first need to have ongoing curiosity about your mate. Be curious about how their day was, what their goals are and how you can help them reach them, and whether they're feeling fulfilled. You should have undying compassion for your lover in everything you do and say. Think about the direct and indirect impact your words and actions have on them and how you want them to feel. Lastly, being consistent with your acts of service, displays of affection, and loyalty are a surefire way to maintain the passion in your relationship.

Below, you'll find some simple tips for sustaining these three vital elements in your relationship.

1. **Avoid adopting a thrill-seeking mindset.** Try to remember that thrills are temporary and the excitement associated with them is fleeting. If you have the mindset of seeking thrill after thrill, you'll quickly grow bored in any relationship. Instead, find the joy in each moment of being together and build from there. On date night, try to recreate some of your fondest memories from the earlier and more passionate stages in your relationship. Is there a restaurant or park you visited that you named as "your spot"? Go there and try to remember what made you fall in love with one another.

2. **Embrace that you don't know all there is to know about your partner.** It's impossible to know everything about anyone because we are all evolving creatures. Our goals, dreams, and

outlook change daily. So you should avoid approaching interactions with your partner with the mind frame that you already know what they're going to say and how they're going to react to you. Instead, force yourself to ask questions in order to learn more about them. There are a number of ways to go about this, such as having stimulating conversations on current events, asking them about their dreams, discovering more about their goals, inquiring about their hobbies, and asking them for stories from childhood. No matter how you choose to attain more knowledge about your partner, being a good listener is key in order to dive deeper into getting to know them. Become a better listener and more invested in learning about your partner. The payoff is gaining an intrigued mate and a more interesting relationship.

3. **Find new and exciting things to do together.** If you spend enough time learning more about your partner, you'll discover some things that you each have yet to experience. Doing something new together creates fresh memories and deepens your bond and mutual interest in one another. You may want to get a tattoo, learn how to jet ski, parasail or scuba dive, go zip lining, or travel to a foreign country together. Whichever you choose, having fun and living in the moment will give your relationship the boost it needs to rekindle the romance.

4. **Switch it up!** Do something that your partner isn't expecting. It's fun to keep them guessing and on their toes (in a good way, of course). Have fun and schedule an out-of-the-ordinary date or experience to intrigue your spouse/partner and recreate interest. Consider scheduling an entire evening and buy them a new outfit to wear for the occasion. Change up your daily routine so that you're giving each other massages with champagne instead of just heading straight to bed. Or if you plan to go to the bedroom, you can always have a blindfold and some toys and props available. And, while you're at it, try out some new positions. I'm sure they will be pleased and appreciative.

5. **Role play.** Go out for date night and pretend not to know each other. Approach your lover at the bar and carry on a

conversation as if you don't know them. Flirt and have some sexy small talk before deciding to leave together for a rendezvous. Throw predictability out the window and focus on discovering your partner all over again. This will open up opportunities to tap back into the desire that brought you together in the first place.

6. **Interview your partner.** Each day, ask your partner, "What's something that made you laugh or smile today?" If you get tired of the same old answers, stop asking the same questions. Start off by sharing a funny story of your own and set the positive tone. Remember, you have the ability to vibrate higher and reap the rewards of your own positive efforts. Lead and they will follow and likely forget their own troubles. It's much more desirable to laugh and smile than to remain upset.

7. **Have more "just because" moments.** Send flowers, write a love letter, or slip a note into their purse or wallet to impress them all over again.

Remember that you both are in your relationship by choice. Be intentional with every single moment, word, text, and opportunity.

TOPIC TWENTY

Self-Care

This section will be brief, but it is still very important.

As a child, I remember my mother locking herself in a closet and sitting in there for long periods of time. My siblings and I would come by and knock on the door and she wouldn't respond. I remember wondering why she did that. Didn't she want to spend time with us? Why was she isolating herself? In hindsight, I now fully understand my mother's need for doing this.

It is very simple to lose ourselves while in a committed relationship. We often place the needs of our loved ones before our own, thinking that's the best way to show love and loyalty. We put our needs last and often don't get to them because we are too tied up with caring about how our value is measured and our worth is perceived. I'm here to tell you right now–if this is you, please stop this unhealthy behavior right away. There is nothing to be gained from neglecting your own needs for someone else's.

If you do not focus on securing what you need in order to be the best friend, lover, parent, and child you can be, every other effort you make will be in vain. Take the time to invest in your own self-care for your benefit and for the benefit of those you love the most.

If your partner needs time alone to recharge and process their situation, please don't make them guilty about it. As I mentioned earlier, we all handle stress differently. Whatever is weighing them down can easily consume them if they do not replenish their energy. Appreciate their desire to create alone time because it will make your relationship stronger. Take the time to miss each other. Time apart is not only healthy, but it's necessary. While they're doing them, find the time to focus on the things that make you happy. Recognize that both of you may be dealing with separate challenges that require time to work through.

Last but not least, make an effort to schedule at least one separate mental health day a month. On this day, you each can spend it how you see fit. If you want to catch a movie or lunch alone, read a book, attend a workshop, or hang out with friends–find a way to release your tension and recharge apart from one another. It can be just as important as date night because it allows you to embrace your individuality and revisit the components of your own identity.

Self-care is *not* selfish. It is needed to sustain relationships. Make it a regular part of your routine and you will find yourself looking forward to it each month.

SECTION IV: YOU BETTA RECOGNIZE!

This section is designed to help you recognize signs that may prevent you from advancing in your relationship. The relationship red flags topic covers common behavioral patterns you should look out for while entering a relationship.

When we find ourselves in new relationships, or even when we become comfortable in our relationships, we may ignore some of the telltale signs that are presented to us. Don't worry, I'm here to give you lovebirds a heads up on when it may be time to start jumping ship.

The Relationship Red Flags are meant to guide you toward recognizing what may be a sign of bigger issues to come and can also help you reexamine the boundaries you have set for yourself and others while in a relationship. I encourage you to reflect and develop your own red flags in addition to this list to ensure your relationship is on the right track.

The What Did I Sign up For section challenges you to think about all the possibilities of what you may be signing up for by getting involved with someone before you actually take the plunge.

So, family, please get ready to take off your rose-colored glasses for a second and take a long, hard look at what is right in front of you.

TOPIC TWENTY-ONE

30 Relationship Red Flags

When the writing's on the wall, will you open your eyes to see it?

Let's spend some time exploring some of the red flags that we may observe in our relationships from time to time but don't always act upon. Some of the more common reasons we choose not to react when we see some of the danger signs early on in our relationships are that we hope things will work themselves out, we choose to minimize the issues, or we simply fail to acknowledge that the issues even exist. Whichever the case, I will share some glaring red flags that should stop you in your tracks and cause you to reflect on the direction your relationship is headed. If you are experiencing two or more of these signs in your current relationship, it is time to re-examine its path and redirect it as soon as possible.

These red flags lie outside of the obvious ones, such as abuse—verbal, emotional, or physical—from your partner, serious addictions that are life-threatening or harmful to their well-being, and other telltale signs. We will discuss the more subtle signs and why it is vital to address them once they rise to the surface.

Choosing your mate for self-serving reasons. I'm going to spend some time on this one because it's critical. Think about the very first time you meet someone. Of course the way they looked and how they carried themselves was a large part of how they caught and retained your attention. Now, let's move on to what happens after a few dates and phone conversations. This is when you decide if this person is still worth your time. If your focus remains only on their appearance, possessions, or swag, you should ask yourself if you are interested in them for the right reasons. Are you heeding to the warning signs they're giving you or blocking them out completely?

A real king listens to his counsel as well as his queen because he knows he doesn't have all the answers. He knows that he has selected his queen for a reason. He must actively and openly seek her advice. If she is to be his rib, she is expected to know things that he doesn't. If Christ is leading him, the Holy Ghost will give him discernment and his queen will often have the same wisdom.

For this reason, you must learn to trust each other at all times. When doubt enters the decision-making process you should be able to seek counsel from your partner and right hand. If you are the primary decision maker in the relationship, you should be confident when including your partner in your decisions. If you are the supporting partner, your mate should be equally open to hearing you out. If you are equally yoked—which is the ideal scenario—and you chose your partner for the right reasons, then they are more likely to possess gifts from God that you do not have.

It is important to remember not to lose your identity while in a long-term relationship. The relationship does not define who you are. Therefore, walking away from a relationship may be the main reason people are at their happiest point right now. A successful relationship does not always thrive as a result of pouring in endless effort. Sometimes you have to take note of the red flags that present themselves and cut ties to avoid wasting your time.

When you or your partner lies about something silly. Lying is never cool, but when someone tells a white lie, you can only imagine what else they will lie about. This causes distrust and resentment, leading the other to second guess everything they are told until the root of the issue is addressed.

They never talk about their kids. Parenthood should be a pretty significant part of your life. Regardless of the age, if a healthy relationship exists between a parent and their child(ren), it will be evident after a while. If you have been seriously dating someone and they confirm they have children but never bring them up, this may be something you want to explore further. Could it be due to a failed or dysfunctional relationship? If so, what does that tell you about your partner? If this is something you care about, ask the appropriate questions and remember to withhold judgment and listen carefully.

Your conversation only revolves around sex. If you struggle to have intimate conversations with your partner to discover more about who they are and find that you rarely see eye-to-eye on anything outside of the bedroom – there may be an issue. Lacking common ground with your partner may mean that you don't have much going on other than a strong sexual chemistry. This should not be #relationshipgoals, and if it is, your relationship lacks depth. If you are looking for more than sex, and can't hold a decent conversation, you may want to start looking elsewhere.

They are never available to talk on the phone while at home. At one point or another, we have all come across this type of situation – either firsthand or through a friend. The personal interaction is on point and everything is all good – until they're out of your sight. Then they go AWOL on you. Communication is limited to text only and you can't get an answered or returned call. This is a textbook indicator that your lover either lives with someone they are involved with or may even be married. Pay attention to what times they don't respond to your calls or texts outside of work hours. Is there a consistent pattern? Don't sweep this one under the rug. If you have assumed your relationship is monogamous and notice the signs, address it right away.

They invite you for an evening out, then expect you to split the bill. Now, I may be a little old school, but I find this one not only awkward, but incredibly rude. If you are a female who is asked out on a date, you should not have to touch your wallet for anything that evening—unless, of course, you choose to. Being forced to go Dutch, especially on a first date, is not a good way to start off a relationship. If he or she wants to spend time with you and is low on cash, this should be addressed up front. Any other way of handling that is just plain tacky.

They badmouth their child's mother or father out the gate. Openly bashing the parent of their child is not a good look – regardless of what has transpired between them. It speaks volumes of their character, as well as their lack of respect of their potential relationship with you. Steer clear of people who don't know how to use a proper filter, especially early on in the relationship.

They repeatedly fail to express how they feel. As mentioned earlier in this section, effective communication is a journey. We all have our own shortcomings when it comes to perfecting our communication within various facets of our lives. However, habitually poor communication can create a serious strain on any relationship. If your partner isn't telling you how they feel, they are likely expressing it in other ways: be it by their actions, during conversations with others, or by internalizing it. Any of these scenarios can potentially be detrimental to the relationship if they continue to block you out.

It's just not working. Once you have tried everything you possibly can to make the relationship work–including humility, honesty, counseling, and compromise–and you find that your partner is not willing to budge or you are not getting the results you desire, it may be time to move on.

It's no longer worth the effort and time invested. If you feel you would be much happier alone, you need to leave. If you notice that therapy with your pastor or counselor has not had the desired effect on your relationship, you may need to come to terms with the fact that you are not compatible, that one of you has given up, or that now is not the right time to pursue or continue a relationship with that person.

The interest to move forward no longer exists on one or both sides. Relationships are not 50/50, they are 100/100. So, if one of you is left providing all of the reasons you should stay together while the other is giving all the reasons you shouldn't, something is seriously wrong there.

You're no longer excited about your future with them. You dread spending time with them. You're not motivated to put in the work. You don't like who you've become. You're not a better version of yourself with this person. Your loved ones don't recognize you anymore.

You believe you would be much happier alone. Without even thinking about being with someone else, you realize you prefer to be alone. You long for solidarity and the peace that being without your partner will bring to your life. If you find yourself feeling this way, it may be time to do some self-examination to be clear that you've done everything you've needed to do in your relationship. It's never okay to use this as an excuse to run out on your family, responsibilities, or commitments. Give your relationship the respect it deserves by taking accountability for your role and all that it entails. I urge you to look within yourself to make sure you've done all that you can do before choosing to leave.

You're sticking it out because you believe it's the right thing to do. You're staying in it for your children. You're concerned about what others will think about your decision to dissolve your relationship. You believe that you've been committed or married for too long to separate and people are looking up to you. You feel like you need to prove the naysayers wrong and try to work it out. These are all the wrong reasons to remain in a relationship with someone. You are not benefitting from this and neither is your partner.

You feel like you've reached the peak in your relationship. You know what they say about everything that has reached its highest altitude. "It can only go down from here." If your relationship is at a point where it's as good as it gets and you realize that you want more for your relationship, this should be taken seriously. Maybe you want to get married or have a child and your partner does not want to. If you're happy, but can't see yourself staying in a relationship with someone who doesn't share your goals, then you should leave. This all goes back to setting the proper expectations in the beginning of the relationship and being clear about your short and long-term goals.

You feel you have outgrown each other. There is nothing more to offer each other in terms of growth and growing stronger together. If you find that you cannot agree on your collective short and/or long-term goals, or the two of you are evolving in different ways and moving in different directions, then this is a red flag that cannot be ignored. The inability to resolve your issues on your own or via counseling is a sign that a discussion of moving on from one another may be needed.

Extreme paranoia or unwarranted strong distrust is displayed. Now, we're not talking about your typical case of possessiveness or jealousy. It's safe to say we have all experienced this at one point or another. Extreme paranoia is a lack of respect for privacy and an aggressive behavior built around mistrust. This behavior may be exhibited in the form of going through your partner's phone, checking their emails, and accusing them of cheating when they haven't given you a reason to do so. Even if there is a history of infidelity or dishonesty in the relationship, the choice to remain there should be coupled with desire to improve the situation. If you find yourself displaying this behavior or you are with someone that does, my advice is to attempt to work it out, but set a time limit. If you find you can't reason with this person at all or you can't stop this behavior after a set period of time, move on.

Selfishness. If you or your partner are selfish individuals, this isn't the end-all-be-all. Recognition of this fact is the first step in correcting or modifying this behavior. But the more this cycle continues, the more resentment grows on the other end of the relationship. Even if you are a selfish person, your love for the other person will always be more than enough to motivate you to change. If not, or if your partner does not change, two of you may not be compatible.

Withholding Sex. Ring the alarm! If this is happening on a continual or continuous basis, there is a major issue here. Sexual intimacy is key for the expression of the love you have for one another. Essentially, it is another way of healthy communication. If there is a pattern of refusal at any time, conversation is needed. Reasons why your partner may be withholding sex may be stress, illness, depression, manipulation, infidelity or it could be due to conflict. As all sex must be consensual, this is your cue to back off with your advances, but also take the time to get to the root of the issue. Talk to your partner and discover what is causing them to hold back. Once you get to the heart of the matter, or if you later find this is a repetitive issue, figure out a way to help them find a healthier way to communicate their issues with you. There is only so much of this type of behavior one can or should tolerate.

Radically changed or secretive behavior. If, all of a sudden, your partner's disposition has changed in a drastic way—from grumpy to overly cheerful, from affectionate to distant, from a sex machine to a prude—beware. An impulsive change of mood without any type of justification is rare. The same goes for a heightened sense of secrecy. If you notice that your partner is suddenly actively guarding their phone, being elusive about their evening or weekend whereabouts or plans, or is ending conversations when you walk into the room…well, you know the rest.

They say they're allergic to latex, polyurethane, and lambskin condoms and have issues with virtually all types of contraception. They refuse to utilize prophylactics and insist they are on the pill, have been fixed, or will pull out. "Don't worry," they say. "It will be fine," the say. Until a few months later when you have to make that dreaded visit to the clinic. If you're not interested in having children or contracting an STD, then this is not the way to go, folks. Please don't fall for the okey-doke. Find a healthy way to protect yourselves during sexual intercourse to avoid mishaps or undesired outcomes. While you're at it, get yourselves tested to familiarize yourself with your partner's sexual history and current status.

They cry during sex the first time. No further details needed. If this happens with either gender, you better run, Forrest!

They display no interest in getting to know your kids. This is a telltale sign that they may only be after your approval until they get what they are looking for. Regardless if they are a "kid person" or not, if they are truly interested in getting to know you, they will want to get to know your kids as well. If you have thought enough about this person to bring them around your kids and they are not receptive, take notice. Your kids are an extension of you and a significant piece of the package deal. A lack of interest in getting to know them shows they may not be interested in a long-term relationship with you.

You haven't met their family or any of their friends. There's a saying that home is where the heart is. If you and your partner are not cohabiting, and you haven't met the people they claim to live with or their any of their friends, you have to ask yourself why that is. What would make them hesitate to bring you around the people who are closest to them? If your partner speaks of their family and friends often but have not offered to introduce you to any of them after several months, this may be a cause for concern. You may want to ask more questions to discover why they are reluctant to introduce you to the people who matter most in their life.

There are unexplained gaps in their history. As you are still getting to know each other, it would be foolish to believe that you will know every intimate detail of your partner's history. But as more time passes and you begin discussing things like the schools you attended, past jobs, and exes, their timeline should become a little clearer. If after more time passes, your partner remains vague about certain periods of their life and is resistant to share those details with you, this may be a red flag. If you choose to press things further, use a gentle approach and avoid probing. However, if they remain tight-lipped, you may be better off moving on.

They want to move in with you too soon or things are moving too quickly. You may have noticed that I didn't put a timeline here. It doesn't matter if it's one year, one month or one day. If you feel things are moving too quickly in your relationship, your opinion is valid. The only people who can make that call are the ones in that relationship. If you feel uncomfortable or if things feel rushed, you may need to step back and reevaluate where the relationship is headed.

They are still living with their child's other parent or their ex-spouse for "the children's sake". This is self-explanatory. Co-parenting does not require cohabiting. Cut your losses and move on.

They want you to have sex with them under their mama's roof. Now, I'm not going to down someone who is living with their mama. There's plenty of reasons to live with a parent ranging from being their caretaker to living there temporarily for financial reasons. However, if they are living under their mama's roof and are trying to sleep with you there, that's a different story. My advice? Thank you for asking. DON'T DO IT! Not only is this disrespectful, but it's lowering your standards as well as their expectations of you. Grab a hotel or move the party to your house.

You sense chemistry between them and their child's parent. Before you write this off as being jealous or overly suspicious, take heed to your gut. If you notice your lover acting strange or differently when their child's parent comes around, it's likely not your imagination. There's history there. Although tension and hatred between the two parents is also a red flag, you don't want there to be too much familiarity going on between them in your presence, either. Their interactions should be cordial and respectful. Anything more may be a topic of conversation for later on.

Whatever you decide is a boundary you do not want crossed. I intentionally left this one for you to figure out. Now that you know some of the things to look out for, come up with your own list of red flags that may symbolize a potential issue within your relationship. Don't use this as a pass to nitpick your partner's every flaw, but rather as a tool to contemplate some of the warning signs that you may have missed in past relationships. Your red flags should not create or conjure up problems that aren't really there. The purpose is to determine a list of early signs that may help you and your partner determine a healthy form of communication that builds trust and a solid foundation for your relationship. Good luck!

TOPIC TWENTY-TWO

What Did I Sign up For?

When it comes to selecting a mate, it is important to look past how someone looks and focus more on how they make you feel. How they treat you. How their personal situation and habits affect yours. How their future goals and aspirations will impact yours. It's far more than just hooking up. Hooking up can lead to bringing a life into this world, which can bind you for life.

It is important to know who a person is and familiarize yourself with their choice patterns and decision making to ensure it is compatible with your goals and expectations. Know what you may be getting yourself into by making the choice to engage with them on a physical level. Physical interaction often leads to intermingled emotional, mental, and psychological experiences down the road. So what will that cost you? What are you possibly signing up for by getting involved with this person?

Throughout this book, I've preached about sticking it out, staying together, making it work, and rekindling the romance in your relationship. But I also listed some red flags to be on the lookout for in your relationship and how these signs may be worth paying closer attention to. For the final topic, I wanted to be sure to touch on how to recognize when it's time to go your separate ways.

I would never outright tell anyone to break up or get a divorce. But I will tell you that if your lover is physically abusing you or causing you any type of mental or emotional distress, if they're suffering from harmful addictions, making habitual poor choices or displaying habits that can put you in danger, you should realize that you didn't sign up for *that*. You may have tried all the remedies and solutions you could, but some things are plain *unacceptable*.

No one signs up for a partner who refuses to give the relationship one hundred percent of their efforts. You can do anything less than that by yourself. It's important not to be so wrapped up in saving the investment you have made in your relationship that you don't see the small details and tendencies that can fester and personally bring you down. That's called cutting off your nose to spite your face.

The truth is, self-examination, accountability and growth all start with you. It's important to take a stance of empowerment, maturity, and discernment while in toxic situations like these and recognize that it's not that they're doing those things *to* you, it's that you're *allowing* them to do those things to you. So, when will enough be enough? When will you find the strength to disassociate yourself from toxic behavior or people?

Lastly, when considering whether or not to stay in a relationship, the only thing you should ask yourself is whether you would want your child or someone you deeply love and care about to remain in a similar situation. If the answer is a resounding no, it's time to move on. You can choose to move on until they get themselves together or to move on permanently. But when moving on, I suggest cutting off all ties until you see a change that you are comfortable with. I also want you to know that you are not a failure, a quitter, or a lesser person for leaving. You are just deciding to choose yourself. And when that's the case, you should never have a single regret.

Peace and God's Blessings, Family.

ABOUT THE AUTHOR

Sam Sylk has dedicated his radio and media career to creating an impactful and positive voice for his listeners each day. His prosperous, multi-decade career is due to his devotion to the communities he serves. Born and raised in Chicago, Sam was educated at Kennedy King College and Columbia School of Broadcasting.

Sam Sylk is currently the mid-host on Cleveland's 93.1 WZAK every weekday from 10 a.m. to 3 p.m. The Sam Sylk Show provides a healthy mix of local and national current events and edgy relationship topics during his "Sam Sylk Relationship Hour" segment. Sam provides easy daytime dialogue and his renowned games, "I Got Five on It" and "Rhyme on Time" are favorites among his loyal listeners with opportunities to win prizes. The Sam Sylk show, which frequently hosts celebrity guests, has become a staple in the Cleveland community. Sam provides engaging on-air conversations that enlists his loyal fans to call in for intriguing on-air discussions, interact on social media, and participate in philanthropic community initiatives and relationship events around the city of Cleveland.

He is a published author of the relationship book, *Men Do What Women Allow* and is the proud owner of four chicken and fish chain restaurants throughout the city of Cleveland. Additionally, each fall, his charity event, "Winter Wraps" collects brand new coats for children in need in and around the Cleveland area.

Sam enjoys spending time with his wife, kids, and grandchildren. He also enjoys watching televised sports and has taken up golf in his spare time. Sam has found success to be a direct result of his tenacity, dedication, and faith in God, family, and the communities he has called home.

You can follow Sam on his website www.SamSylk.com or on social media @SamSylk on Twitter, Facebook, and Instagram. Also check out his YouTube channel under Sam Sylk for more relationship topics and content. To book Sam for workshops, conferences or speaking engagements, please send your request to samsylkshow@gmail.com.

Made in the USA
Lexington, KY
04 November 2019

56560994R00085